William Miller

Historical discourse of the Congregational Church in Killingworth

Connecticut, May 31, 1870

William Miller

Historical discourse of the Congregational Church in Killingworth
Connecticut, May 31, 1870

ISBN/EAN: 9783337259648

Printed in Europe, USA, Canada, Australia, Japan

Cover: Foto ©Lupo / pixelio.de

More available books at **www.hansebooks.com**

Historical Discourse,

OF THE

Congregational Church

IN

Killingworth, Connecticut,

MAY 31. 1870.

By REV. WILLIAM MILLER.

New Haven:

FROM PRESS OF HOGGSON & ROBINSON.

1870.

Preliminary Meeting.

AT a meeting of the citizens of Killingworth, April 14, 1870, it was voted to observe with appropriate religious services May 31st, 1870, it being the fiftieth anniversary of the dedication of the church edifice.

Voted, that Mr. Nathan II. Evarts, Mr. Francis Turner, Dea. Lauren Nettleton, Mr. Orlando E. Redfield, and Mr. E. Harvey Parmelee, be the committee of arrangements.

At a meeting of the committee, Mr. Francis Turner was chosen Secretary.

It was voted to invite Rev. William Miller, to prepare and deliver a historical discourse of the Church in Killingworth, May 31st, 1870.

Voted, that Mr. and Mrs. Lyman Stevens ; Mr. and Mrs. Randolph Stevens ; Mr. Francis Turner ; Mr. and Mrs. John Phelps ; Mr. and Mrs. Ambrose Parmelee ; Mrs. Abner Lane ; Mrs. Ellsworth Hull ; Mr. J. Harvey Lane, and Miss Mary Lane, be a committee to superintend the tables.

FRANCIS TURNER, *Secretary.*

At an adjourned meeting of the committee it was voted, to return a vote of thanks to Rev. William Miller, for his able historical discourse, delivered on the fiftieth anniversary of the dedication of the church edifice, and that a copy of the same be requested for publication.

Voted, that a report of the exercises of the day be also published with the address.

FRANCIS TURNER, *Secretary.*

DECORATIONS.

It is proverbial, that the ladies of Killingworth do well whatever they undertake to do. Their taste is correct, so that they have only to put their fingers to the flowers and evergreens, and they stand forth fashioned into " a thing of beauty."

The following ladies were appointed to superintend the decorations of the church: Mrs. William Miller, Mrs. Francis Turner, Mrs. Andrew Griswold, Mrs. Orlando E. Redfield, Mrs. Ralph Barnum, and Mrs. Mary J. Williams.

The Church stands upon a hill, commands a wide prospect, and is sixty-two feet long, and forty-eight wide. At the east end is a recess for the pulpit and platform. There is a gallery on three sides of the house, around the front of which were festooned evergreen wreaths. At equi-distances were set upon the cornice of the gallery front bouquets of flowers, and between them the names of the pastors of the church. Their names were formed of evergreen letters, with the date of installation made in the same manner underneath, the whole surrounded by an evergreen border.

Beginning at the left of the pulpit, the names were as follows:

Seward, 1738; Ely, 1782; Andrews, 1802; King, 1811; Swift, 1833; Bell, 1850; Lyman, 1866.

In front of the pulpit was the name of the present acting pastor,—Miller, 1870. Around the name was a wreath of flowers, wrought by Miss Anna Marsh; and around the whole a more extensive wreath of flowers, wrought by Mrs. Stephen Norton. Upon one side of the desk was a fuschia in full bloom, and on the other side a cactus, full of beautiful blossoms. At the right of the pulpit was an oil painting of Dr. Asahel Nettleton, a native of the town. Over and under it were his dying words, " While ye have the light, walk in the light."

At the left of the pulpit was a large evergreen cross, with flowers interwoven, wrought by Miss Lucynthia Crampton; over and under it were words—the whole designed to read—"Cling to the Cross of Christ."

Over the arched top of the recess was an evergreen wreath, wrought by Mrs. Antionette Lord; and at the cornice of the pillars, two wreaths; one of which surrounded the date, 1820, and the other the date of 1870, these were connected by a chain, the links of which were made of evergreen leaves. This was wrought by Miss Julia A. Turner.

Upon the rear wall of the pulpit, in the recess, were the following inscriptions formed of letters made of Arbor Vitæ:

"Church Organized, January 18, 1738."

"House Dedicated, May 31, 1820."

Not the ladies only, but the young gentlemen took an active part in the work. They were ready at any point to lend a helping hand. J. Novello Hull, Horatio Kelsey, Densmore Parmelee, Sylvester Hull, and others, seemed to vie with each other as to the amount of assistance they could render.

Let us not forbear to express our warmest thanks to our beloved pastor, Rev. William Miller, for his excellent Historical Discourse. The facts he has brought to light—indicating great labor and research—and laid before us in a manner so interesting, will be of great use to us, and to our children after us. He has made us acquainted with the active labors of those who have gone before us, and who were instrumental in laying the foundations of our religious institutions. We have seen, as it were, their dust animated again. They seemed to be in the midst of us, inspiring us with their spirit, and beckoning us onward to nobler deeds.

ANNIVERSARY SERVICES.

On the 31st of May, 1870, a most delightful day, the Congregational Church and Society in Killingworth, celebrated with appropriate religious exercises the fiftieth anniversary of the dedication of their Church Edifice. The occasion brought together a large concourse of people. The house was filled to its utmost capacity, and many stood around the doors and windows, unable to gain admittance.

Some took their seats full three-fourths of an hour before the opening of the services. The people flocked from all the neighboring towns, literally filling the streets with carriages. So large an assembly never before was gathered on Killingworth Hill.

The elderly persons took their seats below, while "the youth and beauty" filled the spacious galleries.

·The services were opened at 10 o'clock, A. M.

The Choir, under the direction of Dea. J. Buell, sung a song of welcome from the platform in front of the pulpit.

Mr. Nathan H. Evarts, Chairman of the Committee of Arrangement, bade all welcome. He said, it had been designed to send invitations to those who had left town, but they were found to be so many that only a general invitation could be given. He extended a hearty welcome to all, to the former residents and natives of the town, to those whose ancestors had resided here, to our friends from neighboring towns, to citizens, and all others, old or young, who had come up to enjoy with us the festivities of the day.

Invocation and reading of the Scriptures, by Rev. S. Hine, of Higganum.

Singing—Hymn composed by Mr. E. H. Parmelee.

1. O thou to whom we pray,
Help us on this glad day,
Thy praise to sing—
O let the Heavenly Dove,
Descending from above,
Fill all our hearts with love
Great God our King

2. Our fathers worshipped thee;
   Now may our offerings be,
      Like theirs received—
   Here in this sacred place,
   They sought thy heavenly grace,
   Hoping to see thy face,
      In thee believed.

3. This temple here they reared;
   Here they thy named revered,
      And loved thy praise;
   Now in thy courts above,
   They sing thy dying love,
   And all thy will approve,
      In heavenly lays.

4. We celebrate this day,
   And here we humbly pray,
      Grant us thy grace;
   As we together meet,
   To worship at thy feet,
   And here our kindred greet,
      Hide not thy face.

5. When we our race have run,
   And all our work is done,
      And we must die;
   May we thy goodness prove,
   Bear us on wings of love,
   Up to thy courts above,
      To dwell on high.

Prayer was offered by Rev. John Todd, D. D., of Pittsfield, Mass.

Discourse.

Anthem sung by the choir who sang the same at the dedication of the house.[1]

Discourse finished.

Singing, by "ye ancient choir," the 132 Psalm, 1st part—sung fifty years ago.

Prayer.

Hymn, written for the occasion, by John Marsland :

To-day, O God, in love draw near,
And bless thy saints assembled here ;
Humbly we bow before thy throne,
To praise the Father, Spirit, Son.

We praise thee for thy wondrous love ;
By it we live, by it we move ;
O may we give to thee alone
All glory for thy mercies shown.

Again to thee, this house we give ;
Here let thy blessed spirit live ;
May all that in this place is done,
Honor thy name, thou Three in One.

Of those who first did consecrate
This house to thee, as heaven's gate ;
Many are in the world of bliss,
A few are travelling yet in this.

May we the race to glory run ;
And when our work on earth is done,
Sing on heaven's peaceful, shining shore,
Anthems of praise for ever-more.

Historical Discourse.

" I will utter—sayings of old, which we have heard,
and known, and our fathers have told us."—Ps. 78 : 2, 3.

HISTORY is a knowledge of past events. In the study of it
we find much to attract, amuse, and interest. It is attractive,
because it represents the ever changing scenes of life, whether
simple, as that of individuals, or combined, as that of nations. It
is amusing, because it gives scope for the play of the imagination,
and because the passions and actions of men are brought out more
distinctly than in the drama. It is instructive, because it points
out the errors and mistakes of men, and hence we are taught to
guard against them, and also what course to be pursued in order
to attain to virtue and position.

Hence History has been styled, " Philosophy teaching by
example." In other words, we may learn from history what to
shun, and what to cultivate, in order to success in life—the life
of individuals, or of nations.

The sources of history are—sayings of old—which we have
heard and known, and our fathers have told us ; and the written
record. I have made diligent inquiry of the fathers respecting
what they have heard of their fathers, and what they themselves
have known.

The Records, too, have been closely examined.

The history of this church is full of interest, and it would
require more time than is allotted to me this morning to present
it in its detail.

I may pass over many important facts, but shall endeavor
to gather up the chief of them and present them in the following
discourse.

I shall begin with a brief sketch of the town, (for Killingworth included Clinton till 1838,) in order to show the rise of

this, as nearly all the first inhabitants of this place came from the South Church, or parish. ·

The Hammonassetts were a tribe of Indians that lived between the Aigicomock—now East River—and the Connecticut. It was not a numerous tribe. They lived, mostly, near the shore, but roamed over these hills as their hunting grounds.

The name of their Sachem was Sebaquanash, or, "the man that weeps."

Uncas, Sachem of the Mohegans, married his daughter, and came into possession of all the lands lying between the Aigicomock and the Connecticut.

He sold to the town of Guilford all the land west of the Hammonassett River, Dec. 27th, 1641. Upon this, a large part of the tribe passed over to the east side of the Connecticut.

There were but few Indians here when the first planters were entered in 1663. The settlement was called by the name of Hammonassett Plantation till 1667, when it took the name of Killingworth, after a town of the same name in Norwichshire, England.

The first settlers were disposed to treat the Indians kindly, and honorably purchase whatever land they needed, as the following record of conveyance will show.

"'These Presents Witness, that I, Uncas, Sachem Mohegan, have hereby sold unto Mr. George Fenwick a considerable parcel of the land, now lying within the bounds of the Town of Killingworth: we, Woncas, and Josuah my son, do by these Presents alienate, assign, and pass over forever all our Right and Interest whatsoever, in any or all of the land, lying within the bound and limit of the Town of Killingworth to the inhabitants there, which I have not formerly sold unto Mr. George Fenwick, and we do by these Presents ratify and confirm this sale to the said Inhabitants of Killingworth—them—their heirs, or assigns, to have and to hold, enjoy and possess forever, free from any molestation by either of us, Woncas or Josuah, or any other person, or persons from, by, or under us, only as we reserve six acres of land on the great Hammock, four acres about the middle of the Hammock, and the other two acres, at the east end of the Hammock, of the best of the land there, and also free liberty to hunt in the woods, and fish in the rivers and harbors, and to make of any trees for canoes; and rushes and flaggs to make mats,—and for the true performance hereof, we have interchangeably set to our hand, this present November 26, in the year of our Lord 1669.

Mark of WONKAS.

Mark of JOSUAH, his son.

Witness:

HENRY CRANE,

NATHAN KELSEY.

Notwithstanding, in these early days the planters suffered many privations, and were exposed to many dangers.

The Indians still hovered round, prowling as beasts of prey. This is evident from the following record:

"At a Town Meeting, March 23, 1675-6:

"It was voted and agreed upon, that there shall be two common fortifications made in the town for places of defence; and, it was also voted and agreed upon, that these places for fortification shall be at Mr. Woodbridge's—the first Pastor of the South Church—and at Andrew Ward's: further, it was also voted and agreed upon, that Mr. Woodbridge and the townsmen, until a Commission be chosen, shall appoint when the persons in the Town shall come into these fortifications, and that they will be subject thereto, and it was also voted, that these fortifications shall be made by equal proportions by the male persons from fifteen years of age and upwards; and it was also agreed upon, that these fortifications shall be sufficiently made and finished within a fortnight-time, and Mr. Griswold and Wm. Stevens are chosen as a committee for to appoint how this shall be done, and to lay out the proportions."

There must have been some immediate apparent danger, or such haste and precaution would not have been required. Probably what gave occasion for these apprehensions was the breaking out of King Phillip's War, or the roaming of Indian scouts, plundering wherever they could meet with the defenceless inhabitants. But there was no attack, or more serious alarm. The danger was quickly over, and all was calm again.

" At a Town Meeting, Apr. ye 7th, A. D. 1676 :

" It was voted and agreed upon, that there shall be no land let or hired out to any Indian, or Indians, within the limits of this town, for the year, under the penalty of twenty shillings for each acre so hired out."

The Planters were not only sturdy men—able and willing to defend themselves, but they were Christian men ;—and hence their first object was to " erect a Meeting House," and settle a godly minister. The first Pastor of Killingworth—now Clinton —was Rev. John Woodbridge.

He remained twelve years with his people, and then resigned, for reasons which, at the present time, are not known. The next fifteen years the church was without an undershepherd. Divisions sprung up which rendered the prospects of the church gloomy. At last God sent them one, who should unite them, gaining their love and confidence.

Abram Pierson was the second Pastor: " a man around whose character and history the shadows of more than a century and a half have gathered, but who has still left memorials enough of his honorable and useful career to secure immortality."

He was appointed Rector of Yale College. Under him the first six classes graduated. A monument now marks the place " near which was given the first instruction under the authority and protection of the College."

He died 1707. About the time of his death the first settlers came north. The stream began to divide, flowing on in the same direction, but in two different channels.

(The History of the South, or " ye ancient Church," my friend, Rev. Wm. E. Brooks, has ably given in his Two Hundredth Anniversary Discourse, Nov. 13, 1867.)

Parting from the thread of his discourse at this point, I take the northern stream which flowed over these hills and through these valleys.

At what precise time this part of the town began to be settled I have not been able to ascertain. It must have been soon after 1700, for in 1716, the following families were here, viz. : Isaac Kelsey, Esq., Dea. Joseph Wilcox, Dea. Josiah Hull, Dea. Daniel Buel, John Wilcox, Joseph Griswold, Nathaniel Parmelee, Ebenezer Hull, Samuel Stevens, and Edward Rutty.[2]

These were soon joined by Solomon Davis, Timothy Chittenden, and Theophilus Redfield. Others followed ; all church-going and church-loving people. This is evident from their attendance at the first or South Church—a distance of from five to eight miles—and also from the fact, that as soon as there was a sufficient number of inhabitants, they formed themselves into a parish, or North Society. How early this people contemplated the formation of a distinct society, cannot be ascertained. Certain it was before 1728, for,

" At a town Meeting, Dec. 12, 1728 :

" Lieut. Joseph Wilcox, Capt. David Buel, Capt. Josiah Stevens, Josiah Baldwin, and Justice Abram Pierson were chosen a Committee to confer with our Northern Neighbors— the farmers—respecting sd farmers embodying themselves by themselves, for the Public worship, and to consider where it may be most commodious and reasonable for a line to be run between sd farmers and the rest of the town."

Meanwhile it appears that the farmers had sent a petition to the General Assembly, for,

" May 7, 1730, Lieut. Joseph Wilcox and Jonathan Lane, were chosen and appointed agents for the Town to appear at the General Assembly at their session in May, the 19 instant, and there to object against the Memorial of divers of the inhabitants of sd Killingworth, commonly called Killingworth Farmers ; requesting that Killingworth may be divided into two distinct societies, and there to show to the General Assembly, the *unreasonableness* of sd Memorial."

No record is made of the success of this committee, while it seems certain that the Memorial was not granted at this time : for,

" At a meeting of the Farmers in Killingworth, Sept. ye , 18th Day, A. D., 1730 :

" It was agreed that we, the subscribers, would again ask the Town of sd Killingworth, that there may be a line between us and the sd town in order to our being a society with the rest of our neighbors, for the reasons hereinafter mentioned : first, we would humbly suggest that our best interests are much exposed for want of it, for, if faith comes by hearing of the word preached, then hearing of the word preached is necessary, and, if faith be a principal qualification in order to justification, and, if faith comes by hearing the word preached, then we hope no good man will deny our prayer; and, if we cannot be a society, we cannot hear the word preached but seldom, and so have not the means in order to faith which makes our case lamentable, which makes us pray for relief, and pray that a Committee may be chosen by you to settle a line as above said, and your Memorialists as in duty bound shall ever pray.

JOSEPH WILCOX,
DANIEL BUEL,
NATHANIEL PARMELEE.
TIMOTHY CHITTENDEN,
THEOPHILUS REDFIELD,
and sixteen others.[3]

The following is the result :

"At a Town Meeting, Dec. ye 4th, 1730 :

"The within Petition was granted, respecting the choosing a Committee, and the Town will defray the charge of the work that shall be done by the Committee that shall be impowered, Provided sd Committee be allowed by the General Assembly."

The Committee chosen were : Capt. James Wardworth, of Durham ; Capt. Samuel Hill, of Guilford ; and Mr. Samuel Lynde, Esq., of Saybrook.

For nearly five years from the above date, no account of any farther proceedings can be found on the Town Records, so that I have no means of learning whether the controversy was carried on or not. Neither have I been able to find the Memorial which was presented, nor when it was presented.

The following is the Act of Organization :

"Att a Generall Assembly, Holden at Hartford, May, 8, 1735. An act Dividing the town of Killingworth, in the county of Newlondon—into two Ecclesiastical Societies.

"Be it Enacted by the Govener, Counsell, and Representatives in Generall Court assem' led, and by the Authority of the same, that the sd town of Killingworth by a line to begin at Saybrook bounds, at a place commonly called ye South East Corner of Pelletiah Ward's farm, being ye proper Southeast

Corner of Capt. Peter Ward's Ninth Division land, and to extend from thence, W. S. West 5° South to Guilford line, shall and is hereby divided into two Distinct Ecclesiasticall Societys; and ye part of sd town lying southerly of sd line is hereby declared to be a Distinct Ecclesiasticall Societie, with all power and privileges proper for such a society, and that such part of sd town that lieth northerly of ye above sd line shall be and is hereby by the authority afore sd, made into one Distinct Ecclesiasticall Society, with all the power and privileges proper for such a Society; always Provided that all lands in sd town, if ye owner liveth in the town Aforesd, shall be taxed for the Defraying parish Charges only whare ye owner or owners of such land do live."

A True Copy of Record.

Examined,   per GORG WYLLYS, *Secretry.*

This part of the town being thus set off into a distinct Ecclesiastical Parish, the first meeting "of ye north or second society in Killingworth was held att ye hous of Ebenezer Hull in sd Society, September ye 25 day, A. D., 1735, Joseph Willcocks was chosen Moderator, Isaac Kelsey was chosen Society Clerk and sworne. Nathaniel Parmeley, and Nathan Kelsey, and Samewell Steevens was chosen a Committey to warn Society meetings as is nedfull."

The Society being thus organized, the divisions of the following Discourse will take the order of prominent and successive events.

I. Pastors of the Church.

"At a meeting held, May 1st, A. D., 1736, Mr. Josiah Hull and Mr. Joseph Willcocks, and Mr. Nathaniel Parleme (Parmelee) was chosen a Commety to gow and discors with Mr. Samuel Eliot from time to time, and to know his mind whether he intends to labor in the work of the ministree or now."

Samuel Eliot was the eldest son of Jared Eliot, Pastor of ye first church. He graduated at Yale College, 1735. He, probably, had the ministry in view, but for want of health did not enter it. He studied medicine, and died Jan. 1st, A. D.,

16

1741, on a voyage to Africa, undertaken for the benefit of his health, in the 26th year of his age.

It was voted, Nov. 5, 1736, that " wee wold hier a minister to com and preach among us this winter coming."

" It was agred and voated, Dec. ye 1, Day, 1736, that we wold hier Mr. William Seward three months with what we have herd him; and allso, it was voted, that we will a low Mr. Seward thurty shillings for every Sabath Day for the hull term of time."

At the same meeting, " Daniel Buel was chose to read and tune the Salm for three months."

Mr. Seward was " hiered" for another quarter at thurty-five shillings " a weak and his keeping allso."

After Mr. Seward had preached here six months, Apr. 29th, 1737, it was

" Voated that we wold hier Mr. Seward for one quarter of a year upon trial, in order to a settlement in the work of the ministree among us."

It was also " voted that we will give three hundred pounds settlement to the minister that we shall agree to settle among us."

There was no distinction between church and parish in these early days. All Ecclesiastical matters were transacted at the same meeting—the society included the church.

" It was voated, July 6, 1737, that we will have Mr. Seward for our minister, if he can be obtained."

It was agred and voated, Oct. " ye 17, 1737, that we will give Mr. William Seward, if he continue in the work of the menesteree, to pay six pence upon the pound in the list anaulley untill his sallery shall amount to one hundred and forty pounds, at the rate of silver at twenty o fur (four) shillings the ounce, as money now goes, and if the money alters to rise and fall with it."*

---

* " At the same meeting, it was voated that wee will sett Mr. Seward a house 34 feet in length; 28 feet in bredth; and 16 feet between ioynts, and to compleat all the stone work and Covering; windo frames, Casments, Dors, and inside joyners woork Excepted, if he lives and dies in ye work of the gospel ministry among us."

Dec. 12, 1737, " Isaac Kelsey, and Josiah Hull was chose a Commete to fall and hew timber, and frame and sit up a hous for Mr. Wm. S ward." " Nathaniel Parmelee and Josiah Parmelee was chose a Commete to git shingels and Claborods and nails and cover sd hous."

" Daniel Buel and Nathaniel Hull was chose a Commete to Didg and Stone the seller and build Chimnes and underpin sd hous."

The house, thus built, and in which Mr. Seward lived and died, stood where Mr. Lyman Stevens's house now stands. The house was burned several years since.

This vote was afterwards somewhat modified, when six pence upon the Pound should amount to one hundred and forty-four pounds: "after that we will give him to the value of one hundred and sixteen ounces of silver yearly."

To these several votes, Mr. Seward returned no answer in writing. They were satisfactory to him, for on the 27th of Dec., 1737, "it was voted that we wold gow down to the first society meeting hous in Killingworth to ordain Mr. William Seward."

The ordination took place Jan. 18, 1738. The "Elders" present were: Rev. Mr. Phineas Fisk, of Haddam, Jared Eliot, of Killingworth, William Worthington, of Saybrook, Abrah'm Nott, of Saybrook, Thomas Ruggles, of Guilford, William Hart, of Say Brook, Jonathan Todd, of East Guilford. These, together with their Delegates, or Messengers, composed the Ordaining Council.

Mr. Seward made the following entry: Those who were in full communion in the North Parish in Killingworth, at the time of my ordination, and of the first embodying of the church there, are as follows :[4] The number was fifty. It would seem from the wording of this record that the church had been previously formed, though all accounts assign it to Jan. 18, 1738.

Thus the Church was organized, and the Pastor settled, one hundred and thirty-two years, four months, and thirteen days ago.*

Rev. Wm. Seward, the first Pastor, was the son of Dea. William Seward of Durham. He was born in Guilford, July 27, 1712. He graduated at Yale College, 1734, and took his second degree, 1737. He was licensed by the New Haven East Association, 1735.

He came to this people in the ardor of his youth, not being twenty-six years of age at the time of his settlement.

At that time the parish was small, but under his labors it

---

* Dec. 5, 1738, "it was agreed and voted, to sit up a scool among us to instruct children in reading and writing."

Sept. 21, 1741, "Lieut. Nathaniel Parmelee and Abijah Willcocks ware chosen a Comete to petition the Town of Killingworth at a Town Meeting, to grant sd 2nd society their proportion according to ye list of sd society of ye money sequested by the general Court of this Colony for the suport of schools in sd Colony.

Dec. 6, 1758. "It was agreed upon and voted, that there should be a Night School kept, upon the same cost and Charge as the Day School is kept."

Thus advanced were our fathers, in respect to education, that, at this early date, they maintained *evening schools*, so that *all* might be taught.

increased and became strong. The people were widely scattered over these hills, and the ways to their habitations difficult, requiring more energy and perseverance than in these days of ease; but being a man of a firm constitution, and of indefatigable diligence, he performed his duties as a faithful steward, a workman that needeth not to be ashamed—enduring hardness as a good soldier of Jesus Christ.

His heart was in the great work of the ministry he had undertaken. He was mighty in the Scriptures, a scribe well instructed unto the kingdom of heaven, bringing forth out of his treasures things new and old.

He could repeat a large portion of the Word of God; his mind was ever intent to acquire "that learning which was least for show but most for service. He was apt to teach. He held the pen of a ready writer.* He was not eloquent, but impressive. He was beloved by his people. "He sought them, not theirs." He made himself servant to the people that he might gain the more. They "generally had a high esteem of him so laboring among them, esteeming him very highly in love for his work's sake. And he had the comfort to see his people generally united in love, 'keeping the unity of the spirit in the bonds of peace.'" This he acknowledges in his preface to his "Two Sermons on Joseph a Type of Christ." He says: "I present them to you as a small token of my endeared love and affection to you, and as a small acknowledgment of your love and kindness to me."

"As a minister," says Rev. Jonathan Todd, in the sermon which he preached at his funeral, "he was really a shining light, and obtained the great esteem of the most judicious in all our congregations. His preaching was solid, his manner grave and serious, his subjects were the great things of God's law and the doctrines of the gospel. He was excellently gifted in prayer, and remarkable for pertinence and fulness of matter upon special occasions.

"A happy concurrence of ministerial gifts and graces rendered him very useful in the pastoral office in his day.

* One of his congregation requested him to preach from Gen. xlv:4, "I am Joseph your brother." The request was made, probably, Thursday evening. The subject—"Joseph an eminent type of Christ,"—was one that interested him. He says, "I considered withal that discourses of this kind would be suitable on a sacrament day, and therefore preached on it the next Lord's day." The discourse fills 48 pages, 12mo, of closely printed matter—all written in *two days.*

"He labored among this people forty-four years. During this long period he was detained from the house of God but three and one-half days, until the last four Sabbaths of his life." During his ministry the church greatly prospered, though at a period when piety was very low throughout the land. There was no general revival during his pastorate, yet he received one hundred and fifty-eight into full communion, and four hundred and sixty-six owned the Covenant. He baptized one thousand three hundred and forty-three in his own parish, and married three hundred and seven couple.

The following entry is found on the Records of the church : "Feb. 5, 1782.—Departed this life in comfortable and firm hope of a better, the Reverend and Worthy Mr. William Seward, first pastor of this church. After having served God and his generation faithfully, he died in the 70th year of his age, and had just entered upon the 45th of his ministry.

He was much beloved and respected among his people, and all his acquaintance, by whom his departure is much lamented."

The second pastor of this church was Henry Ely. He was born at Wilbraham, Mass., May 15th, 1755, and graduated at Yale College—1778—a class-mate of Noah Webster. He preached first to this people during Mr. Seward's sickness. He continued to supply till July 9th, 1782, when he was invited to "settle in the Gospel Ministry." The same day he returned a favorable answer, though he did not fully accept the call. Thus matters stood till Sept. 2nd, when the Society stipulated to pay Mr. Ely 300 lbs. lawful money, as a settlement, and 90 lbs. salary, "silver at 6s. and 8p. per ounce," or wheat at 5s. per bushel.[5] In addition to this, it was voted to "give him sixty loads of wood by the year." Also it was voted "that if the salary was not paid at the time agreed, then interest should be paid till the time of settlement."

These proposals were satisfactory. In his answer of acceptance he says : " Having received an invitation, with suitable encouragement from you, to settle among you in the work of the Gospel ministry : having received the advice of friends and fathers in the ministry, and seeing, as I imagin, the path of duty plain before me, I cannot be disobedient to the intimations of Providence."

He was ordained Sept. 25th, 1782. Rev. Theodore Hinsdale preached the sermon. Rev. John Devotion gave the Right Hand of Fellowship.

For eighteen years Mr. Ely's pastorate was pleasant, and the people united and happy. No sign of dissatisfaction appears till a Society Meeting, held Nov. 3d, 1800. Then, "on motion to grant the Rev. Henry Ely a salary for the year ensuing, passed in the negative," by a large majority. The causes of this "uneasiness" are not recorded. The parties could not, or did not, agree. Dissatisfaction became more decided and out-spoken. No "accommodation of views" could be made. Negotiations were entered into, and, when the Society agreed to take his house and land, he resigned, and was dismissed, Feb. 12th, 1801. His pastorate was eighteen years, five months and seventeen days.

He gathered into the church ninety-two: one hundred and seventy-three owned the Covenant. He married one hundred and sixty-four couple, and baptized five hundred and seventy-nine.

After his dismission he returned to Wilbraham, Mass. Thence he removed, the same year, to Rome, N. Y., preaching most, if not all the time, at that place, till 1805, when he removed to "New Connecticut," to the town of Stowe, now in Summit Co., Ohio. In this then very new part of the State, he preached gratuitously in a log school house, till the opening of the war, 1812.

His home was on the bank of Pleasant Lake, from which he was driven by the Indians, with only a very few hours' notice.

He then returned to N. Y. and spent the remainder of his days with his children, though he "continued to preach until the infirmities of age pressed too heavily upon him: maintaining his Christian character and integrity to the end. He loved his calling, and strove to do good while life lasted. He had a serene old age, and a peaceful death." He loved more and more, as age advanced, the teachings of Jesus. He taught more clearly the doctrines of the cross, and enforced more pointedly the practical duties of the New Testament.

He died at the house of his youngest daughter, Mrs. E. P. Braton, in Watertown, N. Y., Aug. 2d, 1835, in the eighty-first year of his age.

Mr. Ely built the house where Mr. O. E. Redfield now lives. It was voted, Dec. 2d, 1782, "that Lieut Roswell Parmelee, Josiah Parmelee, and Sergt. Joseph Griswold, be a Committee to git ye timber and hew and frame a house for Mr. Ely."

Another committee was chosen "to see that ye sellar be stoned, and ye chimney built for sd Mr. Ely's house."

For more than eighty years this house was the home of the pastors of this church. When Mr. Bell left, in 1864, the property passed into other hands, and the present beautiful parsonage was built.

The third pastor of this church was Josiah B. Andrews. He was born at Southington, this State. He graduated at Yale College, 1797, and was class-mate of Lyman Beecher, D. D. He studied Theology with Abel Flint, D. D., of the South Church, Hartford, and was licensed by the Tolland Association, June 4, 1799.

In the year 1800 he was sent out by the Connecticut Mission Society to the southern part of N. Y., and the northern part of Penn. He was gone eighteen weeks and two days, traveled 1,349 miles, preached one hundred and eleven times, attended several conferences, and one funeral, beside catechising and instructing children more than fifty times in a public manner, and frequently visiting from house to house. He rode, at one time, over four hundred miles without meeting with any regular minister.

In this missionary tour he was the instrument of doing much good, in awakening an interest in the subject of religion, and in leading many souls to Christ.

Soon after his return he began to preach in this place. March 1, 1801, he occupied the desk for the first time.

At a meeting of the Society, held May 18, 1801, it was voted

"That we will give Mr. Josiah B. Andrews a call to settle here in the work of the gospel ministry."

"Voted, June 29, 1801, to give a salary of $400, and $1,000 settlement."

To this invitation Mr. Andrews replies:

"The state of things in this place is such, at present, united to my circumstances at this time, that if it should meet with the approbation of the people, I should prefer a delay in giving a decisive answer until the first Monday in December next."

From August to December, Mr. Andrews was absent. (I have not been able to learn who occupied the desk during his absence.) After his return he preached till March 22, 1802, when he gave them a formal answer, accepting the call.

February 25, 1802, the church "voted to give Mr. Josiah B. Andrews a call to settle among us in the work of the gospel ministry."

In his answer he says: "Whereas serious difficulties have of late existed in the church, which have caused unhappy divisions among the people, I have, in time past, thought it not my duty to comply with your request, consequently a delay of almost nine months has been made of this important matter since your call was first given." . . . .

Among other reasons for accepting, he says: "Considering that through the blessing of God, and the effectual workings of his Holy Spirit, there hath been a very serious and uncommon attention to divine things since my first entrance into this place, among both old and young, so that we have reason to hope numbers have been born into the kingdom of Christ, forever to rejoice with him in glory, and viewing the progress of the work as still glorious, but apparently much hindered by reason of a delay of the settlement of a minister, that he may be statedly and steadily with the people;—Under these circumstances, I think it my duty to submit the important question relative to my settlement with you, to the better judgment of a wise and judicious council, which may be called in."

Accordingly he was ordained to the work of the gospel ministry, April 21, 1802.

Rev. Abel Flint, D. D., of Hartford, preached the sermon, from Acts, 28: 31. Rev. David Seldon gave the Right Hand of Fellowship.

Mr. Andrews was a small, short man, very active, and much admired by his people. He was animated and popular as a preacher, and an advocate of "high Calvinism." He was striking in his remarks, convincing in his reasoning. He was sociable as a companion, entertaining in conversation, apt to teach, as those under his instruction can testify.

The church greatly prospered under his ministry. Many built their hopes of salvation upon a new foundation, even faith in Christ. Others were strengthened in their christian character. Many who had lived ungodly lives, were led to the Lamb of God, who taketh away the sins of the world, and found peace in believing in Him.

The character of Mr. Andrew's preaching was doctrinal, with pointed application. He discussed a new class of subjects, those which teach the entire sinfulness of man, and his dependence upon Christ alone for salvation ; that morality and good works were not a sufficient ground for a good hope of heaven. He told them that they were in the hands of an angry God,—at his sovereign disposal. He also taught them that whosoever would repent of their sins, and believe on the Lord Jesus Christ, should secure life eternal.

Some took offence at these doctrines, and hence opposition arose. Better feelings were cherished. Sides were taken. Charges were made involving moral character. His usefulness was impaired. A council was called. Lawyers plead the case, but nothing was proved against him. He was regularly dismissed, April 16, 1811. His pastorate was nine years, wanting five days.

In looking back to these days of trial, and yet days of blessing, I think we must conclude that the influence of Mr. Andrew's ministry, was, upon the whole, good. He awoke the mind and set men a thinking. He started this church in its upward course of prosperity. From his day to the present God has blessed us, and the plain practical teachings of Jesus have been loved.

He admitted to the church one hundred and forty-three ; united in marriage sixty-seven couple; baptized one hundred and twenty-five, and attended one hundred and forty-eight funerals.

After leaving this place, he went to Perth Amboy, N. J. where he became involved in difficulty, and left the sacred office. He then studied medicine, received his diploma from the New York Medical College, 1816. He returned to Southington, and remained there till the death of his father. In 1837 he removed to New York City, practising medicine, and preaching occasionally. He died 1853.

The fourth pastor of this church was Rev. Asa King. Coming soon after, or rather in the midst of the excitement attending the dismission of Mr. Andrews, when feeling. ran deep and strong, when friends and neighbors had been alienated, and when opinions on religious subjects were held widely at variance, it was no difficult matter to harmonize these discordant elements. Particular men are raised up for particular occassions. There is a niche which they only can fill. Such was Mr. King. The friends of Mr. Andrews liked him, because he preached so *much like* their former pastor. The opponents of Mr. Andrews were pleased with him, because he preached so *unlike* their former pastor. Hence, at the very first, Mr. King had the good will of all.

The Rev. Asa King was a native of Mansfield, Conn., the son of Mr. John and Mrs. Elizabeth King. Living at a distance from public school, his early advantages for education were limited. When about eighteen, he united with the church in his native place; from this time he had a strong desire for an educacation. The way seemed to be hedged up. He was in feeble health, and had no funds or friends to aid him, still he made the effort. He qualified himself for a teacher, and taught for more than a year on Long Island. He entered Princeton College in 1795, but for the want of health and of funds he left at the end of the year. He taught in Easton, Penn., and then opened a select school in New Haven, where he remained three years and a-half The ruling desire of his life was to preach the gospel. In the Spring of 1801 he entered the Theological School of Dr. Backus, at Somers. He was licensed by the New Haven West Association, October 20, 1801.

Very soon after he was invited to settle as a colleague with Rev. A. Putnam, of Pomfret. Here he continued nine years, being dismissed in June, 1811.

At a special meeting of the second Ecclesiastical Society of Killingworth, held October 7, 1811. it was voted, "that we give the Rev. Asa King, a call to settle among us in the work of the Gospel Ministry."

"*Voted*, That we will give the Rev. Asa King, five hundred and ten dollars, and twenty cords of good merchantable oak wood annually, for his salary, from the time he shall be settled in the work of the Gospel Ministry among us, until the pastoral and ministerial relation between him and us shall be dissolved."

Having accepted the call,* he was installed, November 20, 1811. Rev. Ludovicus Weld, preached the sermon, from 1 Cor. 3 ; 4, 5, 6 verses. Rev. Dr. Lyman gave the Right Hand of Fellowship.

Upon Mr. King's settlement, all discord ceased—harmony was restored. Old friends that had been alienated forgot the past. Subjects of heated discussion were dismissed, doctrines once distasteful were now cordially believed, so that there was tranquillity in church and society.

It is often dangerous for a minister to settle with so much popularity at first. It is like standing on the top round of a ladder, where the only movement must be a downward one. But Mr. King retained his good standing. He labored on, year after year, strengthening the weak, confirming the wavering, and bringing the whole church up to a higher level of christian experience. When he left Pomfret, a person of another denomination said, "I am glad Mr. King is going away, for his people have been worshipping him." For seventeen years he was respected and loved. His influence in town was great. When the temperance question began to be agitated, being a staunch temperance man, he took advanced ground. Part held with the pastor, and part against him. Exciting meetings were held. In earnest debate, questions were discussed, which at present would awaken no interest at all. The very formation of a Temperance Society separated friends, and caused serious divisions in the church. Under these circumstances Mr. King asked for a dissolution of the pastoral relation. At a special meeting, held July 9, 1832, it was voted,—" To appoint a committee to wait on the Rev. Mr. King, and request him to withdraw his request to the society for a dismission."

The request was not withdrawn, and he was dismissed on the 1st of August, 1832. Mr. King's pastorate was twenty years, eight weeks, and eleven days. During this time he attended two hundred and thirty-five funerals; solemnized one hundred and sixty-six marriages; baptized three hundred and fifty-two, and admitted to the church two hundred and fifty-nine.

From Killingworth, he removed to Westminster, and was

* The church voted, Nov. 4th, That Friday, the 15th instant be appointed as a fast preparatory to the installation. The public service to begin at 1 o'clock, P. M.

installed in January, 1833. He remained pastor of this people for nearly seventeen years. He died December 2, 1849, being nearly eighty years of age.

"Mr. King was a christian man." Said his last companion, "I never knew such a christian. He seldom, if ever, retires at night or rises in the morning without repeating some passage of scripture, or some hymn, and adding reflections upon it. He has much communion with God."

He was a sympathizing friend, and but "few knew better how to offer the consolations of religion." He was a man of sound faith, of unswerving principles. "He took hold of the massive pillars of the Divine Government, and there he stood firmly." His master honored him with a long life, and much success in his ministry.

Rev. Ephraim G. Swift was the fifth pastor. He was born in Williamstown, Mass., August 14, 1782. He was the son of Rev. Seth Swift, who graduated at Yale College, 1779. His mother was Lucy Elliot, of Clinton, (Old Killingworth,) a descendant of Elliot the Indian apostle. He graduated at William's College, 1804, and studied Theology with Dr. Stephen West, of West Stockbridge. He was settled a colleague with Dr. West for nine years. Afterwards he supplied several parishes until he came to Killingworth. He commenced his labors here in Jan. 1833, and was installed Dec. 11, 1833.

Mr. Swift was conciliatory in his character, having that charity that suffereth long and is kind, doing good unto all men as he had opportunity. His ministry was laborious but successful. He sought to win souls for the master, nor did he spend his strength for naught. He admitted one hundred and ninety-eight to the church, baptized two hundred and ninety-six, united in marriage one hundred and fifty-three couples, and attended three hundred and thirty-eight funerals.

At his own request, he was dismissed Nov. 6, 1850, being a pastorate of sixteen years, ten months, and twenty-five days. After his dismission the Society entered the following on its records.

Resolved, "That the effort to secure and preserve peace and harmony in the church and society, the faithful and zealous discharge of all pastoral duties, the earnest and consistent and exemplary life, which have characterized the course of Mr. Swift during his ministration with us, merit and receive our most sincere thanks, and that our best wishes will ever attend him through life."

He died at Buffalo, Aug. 28, 1858. Though among strangers, he received every expression of kindness which his condition required, and died, as he had lived, cheered and sustained by a good hope in Christ of a blessed immortality.

The sixth Pastor was the Rev. Hiram Bell. He was born at Antrim, N. H., graduated at Williams College, 1836, studied Theology at East Windsor Hill, and was licensed by the Tolland Association, 1838.

He was ordained at Malborough, Feb. 17, 1840. After a pastorate of ten years, he was dismissed, and was installed over this church, Nov. 6, 1850. He was dismissed, 1864. He is now acting pastor of the church in Westchester.

Of him and his labors I need not speak, for he is here and will speak for himself. Sure am I, that you will give him a cordial welcome in your greetings to-day. Many whose Christian graces were quickened by his instruction, many who acknowledge him as their spiritual father, many who accepted not the invitation, "Come to Jesus"—which he so often gave—will take him by the hand, and throngs of memories will come rushing back to the heart.

He gathered one hundred and twenty into the church, married seventy-six couple, and attended two hundred and fifty-three funerals.

In the list of the departed, during this period, I find the following sad but honorable record. The names on the Roll call of those who fell in their country's service—are Benjamin Lord, Joseph V. Evarts, Wilson S. Hall, Charles D. Stevens, Erwin Nettleton, Ellsworth Rutty, Edson Stevens, Dennis Nettleton, Samuel B. Hill, Henry E. Barnum, George B. Marsh, Elford Franklin.

Of these twelve, but two lie buried here among their friends. Of the rest, some died of disease, and others from wounds received in battle, and were buried from the hospital. One was killed at Gettysburgh, and was buried with the noble slain. One died within those fearful stockades, at Andersonville, where life was wasted away through sufferings and agony, such as are almost unheard of in the annals of cruelty. Though they lie far away on southern soil, and in graves over which friends never weep, yet their memory is blessed, their names enshrined on tablets never to be effaced.

Thus, looking over our homes made desolate by war, redrawing scenes of social and domestic happiness from which some loved form has dropt out, and recalling those who went out full of life and buoyant hope, but who were never to return ; some falling in battle, some by the way, some in southern prisons, forcibly are we reminded of the words of the poet :

> " New England's dead ! New England's dead !
> On every hill they lie ;
> On every field of strife, made red
> By bloody victory.

> Each valley where the battle poured
> Its red and awful tide,
> Behold ! the brave New England sword,
> With slaughter deeply dyed.

> Their bones are on the northern hills,
> And on the southern plain,
> By brook and river, lake and rill,
> And by the roaring main."

To return from this digression.

The seventh pastor was Rev. Timothy Lyman. He was born in Chester, Mass., graduated at Amherst College in 1844, and studied Theology at Andover Seminary. He was licensed by the New York and Brooklyn Association, 1848. He then went west, and for fourteen years labored there, most of the time as a Missionary of the American Home Mission Society.

He spent one year among the freedmen at the South.

On the 14th of April 1866, he was invited to take the pastoral charge of this church and people. Accepting the same, he was installed Nov. 21, 1866.

Rev. J. S. Dudley, of Middletown, preached the sermon. Rev. J. A. Gallup, of Madison, gave the Right Hand of Fellowship.

He was dismissed March 1st, 1869.

I need not give a definite statement of his labors, as they are all fresh in your minds.

Your present acting pastor preached in this desk, for the first time, March 29, 1869.

II. Meeting Houses.

The spirit of the early settlers was manifested at their first society meeting, held Sept. ye 25th day, A. D. 1735, for it was then voted that it was "necessary to build a meeting Hous."

"At the same meeting Edward Rutty, and Josiah Hull, and Daniel Buel was Chose a Commete to lay a memorial before the General Assembly, in October next, to pray the Assembly to establish a Commitey to affix a place for a meeting hous."

"At an iurned meeting from ye 25, Day of September, A. D. 1735, to ye forth day of November next, at the house of Samewell Steevens at twelve o'clock at none ;"

"Josiah Hull and Joseph Willcocks and Edward Rutty and Theophilus Redfield and Nathaniel Parmelce was chose a commety to wait upon the Gentlemen Commety appointed by ye General assembly to affix a place for a meeting hous for sd Society."

"At the same meeting, John Lane and Nathan Kelsey and Samewell Stevens was chosen a Commety to Meashur whare the Gentlemen Commity apointed by ye General Cort shall think it nedful."

Nov. 18, 1735, it was voted " wee wold be in preparation to Buld an hous thurty feet long, 22 feet in weth, and 7 and $\frac{1}{4}$ betwene Gints, with a Dobel Chimney at one end."

Mar. 25, 1736, " it was voted, that ye society hous agreed to be bult shall be set up about eight or ten rods northeast from ye place affixed for ye sitting of ye meeting hous."

This house, either because it was too small, or for reasons not now known, soon gave place for another. It was occupied as a place of worship less than six years. It was called the " society house," and probably was never dedicated to the worship of God.

Nov. 25, 1739, " it was voted that we will go about building a meeting house for the worship of God this year."

"Also voted that we will build sd honse fifty-eight feet in length, thirty-eight feet in bredth."*

Mr. Edward Rutty, Dea. Joseph Wilcocks, and Josiah Hull, blacksmith, "was chose a committee to buld." The posts were to be two feet shorter than those in the first society. The house was to be enclosed with "sawed cla-bords," and the roof covered with eighteen inch chestnut shingles.

This house was so far finished as to be occupied in 1743, perhaps the year before.

I can find no account of any dedication service, though Mr. King, in his last sermon in the old house, says: "it is now nearly eighty years since it was dedicated.

A vote was passed Dec. 20, 1743, "that ye seats and pues in our meeting house shall be dignified by ye same rules that East Guilford hath dignified the seats and pues in their meeting house."

Both houses stood upon the ledges a few rods south of Mr. David Chittenden's, at the head of "Bear Swamp." The last house faced south. There was a door on the south side, and at

---

* In this connection, the following records are of interest:

In 1730, the South Society voted to build a new Meeting House, and tax all the inhabitants of the town according to their list, in building sd house. To this the settlers in this part of the town objected, as they were so soon to be a society by themselves, and would, of necessity, be at the expense of building a house in which to worship. An adjustment was made.

"At a Town meeting, January ye 15, A. D. 1731,—It was voted that our Northern Inhabitants should join us in building a new Meeting House, and that it shall be built by a Rate or Rates particularly by themselves, and when sd Northern Inhabitants shall be set off, and qualified according to law to be a society by themselves, and shall be a Building a Meeting House for themselves, that then, we that remain, that is to say, the old society, shall reimburst back again to those that then will be our new society as much as sd society shall disburst towards building sd meeting house in the old society."

Turn we now to the records of the new Society. Take the following, the last of a series of the same kind. It bears date of Dec. 11th, 1739.

"This society now takeing into consideration the affairs respecting the money payed by the Inhabitants of this society towards building a meeting House in the South or first Society in Killingworth, which money hath not yet been payed to us altho we are now in Building a meeting House in this Society, and tho we have used endeauvrs for the gaining sd money, yet we are still delayed to our damage; Whare fore, by a major vote of this society, Isaac Kelsey, Lieutenant Nathaniel Parmelee and Nathan Kelsey, are now Chosen a committee, to ask, demand, Resieve and Recover of the Inhabitants of the sd first society what the Inhabitants of this society advanced towards the building of the sd meeting House in the sd first society.—all of which is secured to us by the vote of the Inhabitants of Killingworth, assembled in a meeting upon ye 15th day of January, A. D. 1731.

Thus, I presume, the money was refunded after a delay of more than eight years; for there is no further account of the transaction.

the east and west ends. There were nine windows on the front side, and five on each end, and eight on the north side. There was no steeple on the house—it looked like a large, high barn, full of windows. It was for many years a peach-blossom color, but when old and ready to decay, it assumed a "dark brown." The step-stones were low, broken, askew, and rocking. The window casements rattled in the wind.

The pulpit was on the sides of the north, with a large sounding-board over it: square pews below, and galleries all around. The church was surrounded by quite a number of Sabbath-day houses, "where the people gathered at noon for shelter, or warmth, or to eat, or to talk, or to gossip, or, *perhaps*, *all*." These have all crumbled and gone. Shrubs now grow where once the house of God stood. Mr. David Chittenden has kindly, at my suggestion, chiseled upon a large flat rock, which was under the old meeting-house, "1739 and 1820," so that the present and future generations may know where our fathers worshipped.*

The society voted in 1816 to build a new house of worship. This building was raised in 1817, completed in the spring of 1820. On the last sabbath in May—the 28th—1820, worship was held for the last time in "ye old meeting house." Here, for eighty years, the people had gathered. Here had many dedicated themselves to God. Here had more than two thousand children been consecrated to the Lord in baptism; but with joyful hearts did they look towards this—their new house of worship.

As we look back to the old sanctuary which our fathers loved—which they honored with their presence—in which they worshipped—the words of the Psalmist are naturally suggested—"The Lord shall count, when he writeth up his people, that this man was born there." Mr. King's closing discourse was from John 14: 31,—"Arise, let us go hence."

On the 31st of May,—fifty years ago to-day, was this house dedicated to the service of God. The text was in Haggai, 2: 9, "The glory of this latter house shall be greater than of the former."

This house, thus dedicated to God, God has owned, and has often shown his glory in it. Here he has met his children. He

---

* I would suggest that a large stone be placed where the first society house stood, with the dates of 1736—1742 chiseled upon it.

has heard their petitions and granted their requests, even giving them more grace. He has enlarged their hearts when they ran in the way of his commandments. He has honored his servants who have here ministered at the altar, in making them the chosen instruments of leading many to the Lamb of God, who taketh away the sins of the world.

As in days past, so in generations to come, may this house stand—not as a land-mark to guide the sailor outward bound—but as a beacon light, along a dangerous coast, to guide those who are crossing the ocean of time, to the haven of peace, of eternal blessedness.

May the glory of the future of this house be greater than that of the past. May it be a place where God reveals his name that it may be there forever.

III. Seasons of Revivals.

At the close of the last century, the standard of piety in our churches was not very high. The *half-way covenant,* i. e. " a creditable profession of godliness is not necessary to full communion," was generally adopted, and nearly all were thus brought in. A good moral character, and the practice of general Christian duties, were sufficient to admit to full communion. No doubt there were true earnest Christians in those days, but piety assumed then a very different type from that of to-day.

After the time of Whitfield, seasons of refreshing from the Lord were infrequent till the close of the century.

The opening of the present century was marked by great religious movements throughout the land. In 1799 and 1800 many churches in this state were refreshed. In 1801 and 2 there was a more remarkable outpouring of the Spirit. Among those highly favored of the Lord was this town. In the spring of 1801 Mr. Andrews came to preach to this people. Seriousness at once began to prevail. Some of the young people requested their pastor elect to preach a sermon to them on election day, a thing so unusual that Mr. Andrews declined. But the solicitation being renewed, another day was soon appointed. The house was crowded. Many wept. The Spirit of the Lord was working secretly in their hearts. In May, the interest became general, and so continued for several months. In August, as Mr. Andrews was to be absent several months, he invited all who were interested, to meet for religious conversation. More than two hundred were present, "anxious about their salvation." In Sept., 1801, Rev. David Huntington received thirty-two into the church.

After Mr. Andrew's return, the interest was renewed, and, in 1802, seventeen were added to the church. The next year, 1803, "the attention of both old and young seemed to be unusually excited again, and thirty-three were added to the communion." In 1804 twenty-one were added to the church, making, in all, one hundred and three.

"Many lost their former hope, and were led to build again on another foundation, which is Christ, formed in the soul, the hope of glory."

The influence of this revival was great. It reached all classes, soothing bitter feelings, causing animosities to cease, so that all once more enjoyed sweet communion together, unitedly praising the God of their fathers.

Another influence of this revival was, it changed the taste of this people as to the truth they desired to be taught. Instead of smooth things, "healing the hurt of the daughter of my people slightly, saying, Peace, peace, when there is no peace;" they loved solemn, pungent truths, those that take hold of the heart, those that teach that we are all sinners before God, and that there is no hope of salvation, only through Christ, the sinner's friend.

Among those who united with the church at this time were Philander Parmelee and Asahel Nettleton. They were friends in early life, and the friendship thus formed was never broken. They were class-mates, and, I think, room-mates in College. They graduated at Yale College, 1809.

Mr. Parmelee was first settled at Victor, N. Y., May 5, 1812. Dismissed Dec. 28, 1814.

He was settled at Bolton, Nov. 8, 1815, and died there Dec. 27, 1822. He was a laborious and earnest worker. He loved his Master's cause. He was a faithful under-shepherd. Though cut down in the prime of life, he had not labored in vain, nor spent his strength for naught.

Mr. Nettleton studied Theology with Rev. B. Pinneo, of

Milford, and was licensed by the New Haven West Association, May 28, 1811. He entered upon the work of the ministry with his whole heart. But few have equalled him in effectiveness, while at the height of his power and of his usefulness.

Dr. Bacon says: "The power of his preaching consisted very much in the clearness with which he exhibited and urged the duty of impenitent sinners to repent immediately, notwithstanding their dependence on the saving grace of God, and notwithstanding the metaphysical difficulties about the doctrine of the will. While he insisted on the inability affirmed in these words of Christ, 'No man can come to me except the Father who hath sent me draw him,' he also insisted on the New England distinction between natural inability and moral, and made his hearers realize that the 'cannot' is only an obstinate 'will not.' "

As a man, Dr. Nettleton was sociable, and always had power to interest, especially the young. He was a lover of poetry, and would often enliven conversation by introducing a striking passage from some favorite author.

As a preacher, he taught practically the great truths God has communicated to us in his word. He presented truth with remarkable clearness and pungency. He seemed to know just what topics to select, and when to urge them. He was never afraid to make a faithful application of God's word to the heart and conscience, or to bring it to bear upon any known course of sin.

"His manner in the pulpit, and in all his dealings with individual inquirers," says Dr. Bacon, "was intensely solemn, and in that way impressive; while now and then there was something like 'sign-language' in his gestures, and, corresponding with it, something imitative in his tones." He adds, "The brotherly regard and respect which Dr. Taylor and Dr. Beecher had for him, to the end of life, is a better tribute to his memory than any eulogism that could be written."

Dr. Todd says, "I heard him preach what was said to be his first sermon. It was in the school-house on Parkershill. I recall that sermon—it must have been sixty years ago—about Balaam and Balak. I remember the preacher was very awkward. He would bend the knees, as if making a courtesy, every few minutes. How different from the same man when I met him in 1820, at the revival in Yale College, when he seemed almost to raise the dead. No one who did not hear him in those days can have *any* idea of the simplicity, keenness and power of his preaching then. His throne was in the school-house meeting, crowded, dimly lighted. breathless and solemn. It is a great honor to Killingworth to have raised one such man."

He died at East Windsor, May 16, 1834.

In his last sickness, near the close of life, one said to him, " You are in good hands ; are you willing to be there ?" He replied, " I am, I know not that I have any advice to give my friends. My whole preaching expresses my views. If I could see the pilgrims, scattered abroad, who thought they experienced religion under my preaching, I should like to address them. I would tell them that the great truths of the gospel appear more precious than ever, and that they are the truths which now sustain my soul."

Among his last articulate utterances, was an allusion to a farewell sermon he preached in Virginia, from the words: " While ye have the light, walk in the light."

At eight o'clock in the morning of a beautiful May day, he calmly fell asleep in the arms of the Savior he loved.

May we all remember his dying words, " While ye have the light, walk in the light;'' and, in order to do this, "cling to the cross of Christ."

In 1810 God again visited this people, and fifty-one were gathered into the church.

I see before me two, who, sixty years ago stood up in the old church and avouched the Lord to be their God and Savior. Throughout this long period their testimony is "There has not failed one word, of all his good promise, which he promised by the hand of Moses, his servant."

In August succeeding the dedication of this church, in a Bible class taught by the pastor, commenced " *that ever-to-be-remembered revival.*" " It had been," says Mr. King, " in pleasing progress for some time, when, under the labors of Dr. Nettleton, it received a new impulse, and went forward with unusual power." Dr. Nettleton says that, " on the 25th of Sept., 1820, he attended an inquiry meeting at which sixty-two were present. On the 29th, thirty-nine were rejoicing in hope, and on the 23d of October there were ninety rejoicing." Mr. King says that "the hopeful converts were one hundred and sixty-two."

The influence of that revival upon the church was very happy. It produced unanimity of sentiment on doctrinal points about which they had long contended, and cordiality of feeling, where there had been prejudices of long standing.

There are many present here to-day, who remember the impressive scene of Jan. 21st, 1821, when one hundred and seven stood in these aisles to profess their faith in Christ. A deep feeling rested upon every heart, almost like the felt presence of God. It was not the moistened eye, but the breathless silence which told of feelings too deep to be uttered.

These are some of the sayings in regard to this revival which we have heard, and our fathers have told us.

Beside these, there have been other seasons of the gracious out-pouring of the Spirit. In 1827, forty-nine were added to the church; 1830, twenty-two; 1835, twelve; 1836, fifty-nine; 1843, seventy; 1847, twenty-five; 1854, forty-one; 1858, forty-six; 1866, fifty.

"These years are memorable in the annals of this church, and glorious in the eyes of God's people." Our borders were enlarged, and we can say, "Behold the tabernacle of God is with men, and he will dwell with them, and they shall be his people, and God himself shall be with them and be their God."

IV. Conferences, Sabbath Schools, &c.

Mr. Andrews says: "In April, 1801, perceiving that the Lord was in a very peculiar manner pouring out his Spirit, and that many were seriously inclined, a weekly Conference Meeting was established."

I have not been able to learn how these meetings were conducted, but they appear to have been meetings for religious conversation and prayer.

At first they were looked upon in an unfavorable light, being regarded as a kind of secret conclave, for party purposes. Insinuations were thrown out, but to no purpose, for those who had established these meetings swerved not from their steady purpose of seeking and glorifying God. But when richer displays of God's grace were made manifest; when, according to the Prophet, "sinners in Zion are afraid, fearfulness hath surprised the hypocrite," when the general cry was: "Lord what shall I do to be saved?" opposition ceased, and these meetings became fully established, and they have been continued uninterruptedly to the present time.

The next upward step was the organization of the Sabbath School.

Mr. King was a live man. His heart was in the work, and whatever would advance the cause of Christ, he was quick to sieze, and find its practical value. In 1816, the first Sabbath School was held. The Pastor, Dr. Turner, and Bro. Reuben Hinckley, were appointed to conduct the exercises. All children between six and fifteen years of age were invited to become members. The lesson was the first twelve verses of the first chapter of the gospel of St. John.

On the day set for the opening of the school, Mr. King and Dr. Turner being both absent, Mr. Hinckley took charge of the school. He gathered the children into the front seats, and then divided them into four classes of about eight in a class. At the opening and close of the school, there was neither singing nor prayer.

Mr. Hinckley, Miss Sally Davis,—afterwards Mrs. R. Hinckley,—were two of the teachers in this first school, and they are with us to-day, with young hearts, though advanced in years.

Subsequently, Mr. Hinckley became the first superintendent, which position he held for twelve years.

His interest in the Sabbath School has never abated. Though now nearly four score, he takes great pleasure in seeing the children gather into their classes on the sabbath, and in listening to their songs of praise.

There are present, this morning, several who belonged to this first school of thirty. Among them is Dea. Abel Wilcox, who was the second superintendent, which position he held for nearly twenty years.

From this small beginning, the school has increased till it has sometimes numbered two hundred and fifty, including not the young merely, but the aged—all who love the study of the Bible. God has blessed the instruction of his Word, for, of those who have united with the church since 1816, a large proportion has been from the sabbath school.

The first or society house had a "single chimny notwith standing ye former voat." Whether this house was ever warmed or not I do not know. But for the second house there was no provision made for warming it. In this region of hills, and snow, and wind, a house with no surrounding trees to shelter, or fire to warm, must have been a cheerless place in which to worship the most High, yet these sturdy men of yore, inured to the cold, here assembled and listened to the words of heavenly wisdom.

I have sometimes fancied Dea. Wilcox, of Tower Hill, Isaac Kelsey, Esq., of Cowhill, Theophilus Redfield, of Chestnut Hill, and Edward Rutty, of Parkers Hill, all going to church, probably on foot, from three to four miles, through a keen, cold, blustering storm of mingled snow, and sleet and rain, and sitting all day, in the old open meeting house, without a fire, listening attentively to the word preached, and being profited thereby. I have wondered at the patience, and admired the faith of our early pastors, when clad in fur, they delivered their messages of love, when the only word that would fire the eye was "Amen," at the close of the service, so that the hearers could go to their "Sabba-Day houses," or to the neighbors to get warm. The internal fire must have been strong and glowing, in order to keep off the external cold, or some would have frozen.

So quiet and still was it around the old house that the sparrows found it a good place to build their nests. The squirrels, also, often disturbed the decorum or gravity of the worshippers, by running from pew to pew, leaping the aisles.

There was once one of the congregation who had leaned his head forward and was fast asleep. A squirrel came running along, when a boy struck it a hard blow, and he fell right on the sleeper's bald head. He suddenly awoke to the amusement of all around. O that there were squirrels in our modern houses to wake up the sleepers.

There have been twelve Deacons. Dea. Joseph Willcocks was the first, and was probably chosen at the organization of the church. He lived to a good old age—a faithful man—one that feared God. Unlike many churches, we have had good deacons, men of principle—of exemplary piety—Puritanic men. They loved the cause of Christ, and were willing, in their turn, to "take the laboring oar."

Eight have closed their labors, and have entered into rest. Four remain to this present.

During the one hundred and thirty-two years since the organization of the church, there have been seven pastors, making an average for each of about nineteen years. Mr. Seward's pastorate was the longest, forty-four years. Mr. Lyman's the shortest, two years and three months.

The first six pastorates averages twenty-one years and eight months.

During the whole history of the church there has been less than two years, in which this people has been without a pastor, or a pastor elect.

It would, probably, be difficult to find another church of which the same is true.

Our fathers ever manifested a generous and noble spirit.

In 1737, the salary voted to Mr. Seward was "at the rate of silver at twenty-four shillings the ounce, as money now goes, and if money alters, to rise and fall with it." Money depreciated. In 1751, silver was 54 shillings per ounce, in 1752, 3 lbs. and 10 shillings the ounce, 1753, it was 4 lbs. to the ounce. Still Mr. Seward received the same value as when silver was only 24 shillings the ounce. In 1751, his salary was 135 lbs., two years after it was 416 lbs.

In 1797, Mr. Ely made a statement that his salary was insufficient to meet his yearly expenses. A committee was appointed. They report: "Your committee are of the opinion that it is highly reasonable that the society should make an allowance to Mr. Ely, on his last two salaries, the sum of one hundred and ten dollars, and this, because from the investigation they found that the general advantage accruing to the community from the high price of things, has operated in the reverse to Mr. Ely, and has made his salary less productive than formerly."

This report was accepted. The society borrowed the money

and paid it to Mr. Ely, and then, at the same time, voted to raise his salary 10 lbs. a year. Thus generously did our fathers act.

There have been trying scenes in the history of the church. The passions were excited, and it seemed for a while, as if the church would be rent asunder, but like some sudden squall at sea, its rage, though furious, was but momentary, and all was calm again.

They had an excellent way of getting over difficulties. Take the following as an illustration.

At a meeting of the second church of Christ, regularly convened at the meeting house in North Killingworth, Aug. 4th, 1808, the following act was passed :

"Whereas great unhappiness and painful divisions have long existed in this church, and whereas the acts of this church in their last three meetings, which were holden with a view to effect a healing, which is now experienced, have not been placed on record, only on file, *voted*, that the pastor now records, only this our final act of oblivion, with respect to all past difficulties, and that we will cordially receive each other in the bonds of the gospel as brethren who are disposed freely to forgive each other, and have by mutual agreement now settled all past differences and layed aside all disaffection that we may prayerfully worship God together, and enjoy mutual faith through our Lord Jesus Christ."

Beecher says: "There is an ugly kind of forgiveness in this world—a kind of hedgehog forgiveness, shot out like quills. Men take one who has offended, and set him down before the blow-pipe of their indignation, and scorch him, and burn his faults into him, and then—forgive him."

Not so here, so complete was the reconciliation that even the parties are not named, not even the cause of dissatisfaction. Oblivion rests upon the whole transaction. May the mantle of the sires fall upon the children, and children's children, for successive generations. " Charity covers a multitude of sins."

It is a striking fact, that from the rural districts, more young men, comparatively enter college and the ministry, than from the villages and cities, where is the restless hum of business strife, and the dissipation of fashionable life.

From our homes, nestling among the hills, there have gone forth those who have occupied stations of trust and usefulness. Fourteen have graduated at college, and two died in their Collegiate course at Yale.[6] Eleven have entered the ministry.[7]

I have already named Philander Parmelee and Asahel Nettleton. Then there was William S. Pierson, the beloved Physician. Dr. John Todd spent his early days with us. That distinguished missionary, Titus Coan, is a native of this town. Here he played. Here he was rescued from a watery grave by a friend and neighbor, who still lives. Here he studied, and how much his character was molded or shaped by that holy man, Mr. King, to whom he recited, I know not. He went from this place when he was about twenty-six years of age. Even in childhood he indicated what the man would be. In his deportment, he seemed to be conscious—not proud, far from it,—that he had a work to do.

He was born Feb. 1st, 1801. He was a child of many prayers, trained by christian parents, and by them taught the fear of the Lord. Though he did not make a profession of religion while in town, yet he was known as a man of religious character, a man gifted in prayer, an earnest worker in the Master's cause. As a teacher in our schools, his influence remains to this present. He made a profession of religion at Riga, N. Y., March 1828. He studied Theology at Auburn Seminary, and was ordained in Park Street Church, Boston, Mass., April 4, 1833. Then he went on an exploring mission to Patagonia. Landed near the straits of Magellan, Nov. 14, 1833. He found everything unpromising, returned, and arrived at New London, May 14, 1834. He was married Nov. 3, 1834, to Miss Fidelia Church. He embarked for Honolulu, Dec. 5, 1834, and arrived June 6, 1835. He was stationed at Hilo. Here his labors have been greatly blessed, wonderful has been the work God has wrought by him. A heathen island has been transformed, and, instead of idol worship, everywhere is seen and felt the pure influence of the gospel of Christ. The wilderness and solitary places have been made glad by him, and the Isles of the sea have been converted to God.

The admissions to his church for twenty-five years, when his connection with the American Board ceased, and his church became a self-sustaining church, were eleven thousand, four hundred and ninety-one.[8] In 1863, his church contained four thousand three hundred and eighty-six members.

Mr. Coan is now on a visit to the United States, the first that he has made since entering the service, Dec. 5, 1834.

V. Retrospect.

Fifty years ago to-day, this house was dedicated to God. How different our situation from that of our fathers! They lived more simple, more frugal than we. They came to church on foot or on horseback, we in cushioned carriages. They "seated" the house of God, we obtain our seats by the highest bid. They "dignified" the house, we know no distinction; seats offered alike to all. They were called to church by a drum, we by a bell. They sat through all the cold winter's day, storm never so hard, without a fire; we have ceiled houses and well warmed.

We, also, are situated different from what our children will be. They in their turn will refer to us, and, fifty years hence, shall we be contrasted with the generation that then is; yet in a great measure they will be as we are. Character, influence, is like many streams, which disappear for a long distance, and all traces of them seem to be lost, but farther on come to the earth again, and flow on to the ocean. So the influence we exert may seem to be lost, but it will rise in a future generation to mold and shape destiny. How often do we hear it said, that a child resembles a grandparent, or even some earlier ancestor. What a lesson this to us, who are now the actors on life's stage.

Standing then, on this pivoted moment, and looking back;—What changes. What desolations hath God wrought? Our fathers, where are they? Where are those whose locks were silvered o'er with age when this goodly temple was raised? Where are those who were foremost in erecting this sanctuary, for themselves and children, in which to worship God? Where is he who then ministered at this altar?

They are gone—all gone.

Fifty years ago these seats were filled with the aged—the young—the beautiful. Their seats to-day are vacant. They greet us only in spirit. They come not to welcome us to their homes any more. The bright, blazing fire casts not their shadow upon the wall. The old armed chair is set aside, and children who are a crown of joy to the hoary head, weep over the graves of their sires. Alas! how many who were then young are not with us now. Not a family circle remains to-day as it was then. Dear ones have fallen every year. Our ranks are thinning, and soon all will be gone.

In this period, how many have been added to the countless dead! Probably not less than two thousand of our townsmen have mouldered back to dust, since the worship of God has been established here, and the voice of prayer and praise have ascended from these heights of Zion.

Of all this number but one reached the age of a hundred.* She was born 1732—memorable for the birth of Washington—and died 1832. She worshipped in all three houses that have been erected here for the worship of God.

Through these years under review, the human heart has acted out its deep depravity, showing how fully it is set to do evil. On the other hand, God has made rich displays of his grace, revealing himself a God, gracious, long-suffering, ready to pardon. He has heard the voice of prayer, blessed the labors of his children, and sent his good spirit to renew and sanctify the heart. Since this church was organized, one thousand and ninety six have taken upon themselves solemn vows, and dedicated themselves to God. The present number of the church is two hundred and seventy-two, so that about eight hundred have been housed in the grave—gone to their eternal home.

> " What is this passing scene ?
> A peevish April day,
> A little snow—a little rain,
> And then night sweeps along the plain,
> And all things fade away,

Whatever else is true, we are swelling the stream of dying

---

* Mrs. Mary Turner, wife of Capt. A. Turner.

immortals, which, ever flowing on, will soon engulf us all, and we
shall rest beside the generations that have gone before us.

What a page in the world's history would the events of the
last half century comprise. Yea, what since this church was
organized. Kingdoms have crumbled. Thrones have been over-
thrown. Wars have desolated our land. The combined force
of the French and Indians has been broken. The oppressive
yoke of foreign power has been shaken off—and in the bloody
strife—thousands have fallen. On the gory field—are they laid—
far from home and loving hearts.

General intelligence has been diffused. Colleges and Semina-
ries of learning have been established. The school houses " where
New England men are made," dot the land. The old beaten
tracks are left. Inventive genius has been busy. Franklin has
" caught and tamed the lightning," and Morse has taught it not
only the " English language," but the elements of all language.
The steamboat plows every river and the mighty ocean. Mountains are levelled and valleys raised, and the steam car speeds
across the continent. Battles for civil and religious liberty have
been fought, and the victory won.

Bible Societies, Mission Societies, Temperance Societies,
have all come into being since our fathers first worshipped here.
Thus marked has been the progress that has been made in sci-
ence and literature, and in all that relates to the extension of
Christ's kingdom since this goodly temple was reared on this
beautiful hill.

Instead of the fathers, shall be the children. They are the
connecting link between the past and the future. Through them
is to be transmitted the rich inheritance we have received. Our
fathers were wise men—far-seeing men. They well understood
that the prosperity of society depended upon the permanence of
the gospel ministry.

Sept. 9, 1736, we find the following record :

" We being set off by the General Assembly, to be a distinct
ecclesiastical society, with all powers and privileges proper for
such a society,—we have therefore agreed and voted that we
will set up and carry on the public worship of God among us
for the future, as God shall enable us."

"Dec. 1, 1736, it was agreed and voted that we will uphold the worship of God among us continually."

From that day to this, there has not been wanting to this people a religious teacher. The fire has not gone out upon the altar.

"The upholding public worship continually"—what a power! It reaches through the whole history of man—the life of the soul. It affects his present as well as his future happiness. It stimulates thrift and enterprise as well as sobriety and decorum. Its victories are not those wide wasting victories of the conqueror, but the noiseless victories of peace and love. Its triumphs are not the triumphs of vice, but of virtue. It raises no "Trajan Pillar," no " Coliseum," erects no granite pyramids, founds no marble College to the exclusion of God, and all that relates to the destiny of man; but it erects pillars of true "glory on Malabar's coast." It builds pyramids of enduring worth—built of living stones and cemented by the blood of Christ, which stand as the proud trophies of the gospel, and will stand when Egypt's fall. It rears Colleges, and dedicates them to Christ and to the church. It sends up the high spire to glitter in the sun and be as a beacon light to the weary traveller, to tell him where is the house of God—that he is safe. It points to the tomb, and farther—it points beyond the tomb, and brings from thence the great and glorious truth—

Man, thou shalt never die.

Its influence is transforming upon the heart and character. " Whereas I was blind, now I see."

It was to enjoy the worship of God and the privileges connected with it, that our fathers left the quiet of their homestead-circles—suffered in prison—braved the dangers of a winter passage, and the severe frost and snows of these New England Hills.

It was for this that—

" A band of exiles moored their barks,
On the wild New England shore."

It was for this that—

> " They shook the depths of the desert's gloom
> With their songs of lofty cheer."

It was for this that—

> " The sounding aisles of the dim woods rang
> To the anthem of the free."

> " Aye, call it holy ground,
> The spot where first they trod,
> They have left unstained what there they found,
> Freedom to worship God,"

It was for this, they levelled the forests and planted vine-yards on these rugged hills. For this they encountered the dangers of an Indian warfare. For this they resisted the tyranny of their mother country, rose to arms and poured their blood in the defence of Freedom. For this they passed through those almost superhuman struggles, to give unto us, their children, those inestimable privileges which we this day enjoy.

Yes, the pulpit made our fathers what they were,—men of sterling character—of stout heart—of ennobling views. They have entered into their rest, and we into their labors. We have come into possession of what the pulpit secured to them : for it

> " (in the sober use
> Of its legitimate and sober powers)
> Must stand acknowledged while the world shall stand,
> The most important and effectual guard,
> Support and ornament of virtue's cause."

The pulpit is the central, moral power of the world. Its in-fluence is abiding. Its work is permanent. The monuments of art crumble. Where is Babylon, with its towering walls and hanging gardens! Where is the splendor of Palmyra! Where is Thebes, with its hundred gates! Where is the kingdom of Alexander! Where are the trophies of Cæsar. They are gone—all in ruins! "Where are the monuments of the work of the ministry! In the ransomed spirits; in the sweet peace of the christian's dying bed; in hearts transformed; in virtues to bloom forever; in souls that are immortal; in the glories of the resurrection; in the crowns incorruptible and unfading; by the river of of life, and amidst the splendors of heaven."

What interest cluster around and in a historic day like this! Old associates are revived, faces once familiar are recalled, homes, as they were years since, are repeopled, and we are young again. We embrace again the rocks and trees, around which we played in early life. We gather again at the paternal knee, and feel again the hand of love resting on our heads, and all the tender feelings awakened by the name of father, mother, arise fresh in the heart.

We go farther. We recall our ancestors. We enter their humble dwellings. We sit at their frugal board. We are with them in their toils as they cleared these hills; in their sympathies as they met to consult about the house of God; in their sacrifices, when with one mind and one heart they labored together for the honor of Christ; and into their joys, when they saw their efforts crowned with success.

This festive day will quickly close. This assembly will part, never all to meet again till we meet at the last day. These flowers will wither. These evergreens will fade; and, when another anniversary shall come, these names will be crowded closer together, and others will be placed upon these walls. In this pulpit, other men will preach. These seats will have other occupants. Others will sing the songs of Zion. Others, too, will sustain the ministrations of this house. May this Church be enriched in everything to all bountifulness. May her love, her faith, her prayers abound!

At the battle of Lake Erie, when one after another of the brave men fell, the survivors looked silently around to Perry, and then stepped into their places. Those who had fallen, wounded and weltering in their blood, were all found with their faces towards him, and their eyes fixed on his countenance.

So when 1870 shall be linked with 1920, may those who are then in the midst of the conflict, see that we have fallen at our posts of duty—each with his eye on the great Captain of our salvation—Christ the only hope of glory.

To-day we would rededicate this church to the service and

worship of the one living and true God. To-day we would re-consecrate ourselves to Christ. To-day we would provoke one another unto love and good works, emulating the bright examples that are before us. Thus may the faith of the fathers be transmitted through us, the sons, to those who shall come after us and worship in this sanctuary. And now, what wait we for! "Arise, O Lord God, and enter into thy rest—thou and the ark of thy strength." And here we, thy people, will abide forever.

Afternoon Services.

At the close of the morning service, all present were cordially invited to repair to the Town Hall for refreshments.

Of the entertainment, we need only say, that it was one of those rare feasts such as the ladies of Killingworth know how to give. Or, as Dr. Todd said of it, "if other ladies thought to provide a better or more inviting feast, than had been provided for them to-day, in this they would be disappointed."

Silence being required, Rev. Dr. Todd invoked the Divine Blessing.

Nearly eight hundred people had their wants supplied.

This was an hour of social regathering, and of mutual greetings. Old friends met again on the Hill and spoke words of cheer. It was an interesting sight to see friend meet friend, and to hear the hum of happy voices,—often the shout of glad surprise.

At two o'clock, all repaired again to the Church. Again the spacious house was filled to repletion.

Mr. E. H. Parmelee gave an Address of welcome, as follows:

ADDRESS.

Friends and fellow-citizens of Killingworth, and friends from abroad, to whom this place is endeared by the remembrance of your fathers, and you from neighboring churches, who have assembled with us to-day, to join in the celebration of this anniversary :—We welcome you to this home of our fathers. We welcome you to this house of prayer, which they here erected, and, a half century ago, dedicated to the worship and service of Almighty God. And we cordially invite you to unite with us, as with grateful hearts we offer prayer and praise to Him whom

4

our fathers worshipped. With what considerate regard for the honor of their Maker, for the advancement of the cause of Zion, and for the welfare of succeeding generations, did they here erect this house of prayer, this temple on the hill, the site of which seems to be suggestive of the thought that their aspirations were heavenward. But I would not wish to be understood as supposing that God or heaven is nearer the hill top, or the mountain top, than the valley. Yet to the mind of the Bible reader, there are many interesting thoughts associated with the thought of ascending an eminence to commune with our Heavenly Father. We remember Moses on Sinai communing with his God, and receiving the commandments; we think of Elijah, who alone was left of the prophets of the Lord, ascending Carmel's heights, there to confront the four hundred and fifty prophets of Baal, and there to decide the question,—" Whether indeed the Lord was God, or whether the supremacy belonged to Baal"; and our faith is strengthened as we think of his glorious triumphs there. We remember Zion, where God's ancient people worshipped. We remember, too, that our Savior went out into the mountains to pray.

> " Cold mountains, and the mid-night air,
> Witnessed the fervor of his prayer"

We think of the scenes of Calvary and Olivet. And with these memories clustering around their minds, we wonder not that our fathers selected this eminence as a site for their house of worship, that they might say to their children, and to their households, " Come, and let us go up to the house of prayer, and bow before our Maker." O what sacred associations are in our minds connected with this place.

Here on this hill for half a century God has fed his flock, and here watered it from the living fountain. Here it has been watched by faithful shepherds. Other shepherds were here before the erection of this house,—viz., Seward, Ely, Andrews,— who are known to many of us only in history, or in the traditions of our fathers. But when we come to the name of Rev. Asa King, the hearts of many of us are warmed with the most tender recollections. He was the shepherd of the flock when we were the lambs of the fold. By his office and ministry many of us were, by our parents, consecrated to God in the sacred ordinance of baptism. From his lips we heard the first gospel sermons of which we have any recollections; and for myself, I would say that the first sermon, the subject of which I remember, was from him, on Ezekiel's vision of dry bones.

I remember too that he was the first king that summoned his people, and marshalled his forces, and led them in person, in a desperate charge upon the army of the subjects of king alcohol; and leading that army in person as he did, the missiles of the enemy falling thick and fast about his head, he received many a grievous wound; yet undaunted, he pushed the battle to the very gates of the citadel of the enemy's stronghold, and many of the subjects of king alcohol deserted his cause, and enlisted in the temperance army; and the ball which was then set in motion rolled on, and the result is, that the enemy has received such a check, that to-day Killingworth can boast that she has not a dram shop in town. And if in any instance any of our inhabitants are found intoxicated, we have the consolation of supposing that they have been to some neighboring town to obtain the means of becoming so.

Next the beloved Swift ministered to the flock. To strangers that name might seem a misnomer; for he was not swift to speak, not swift to adopt new measures or new means; but swift to run to the relief of the suffering; swift to visit the chamber of the sick and dying; swift to aid in promoting every good word and work; but he has gone to his rest, and his works follow him.

Next was heard on the walls of Zion here, the sound of a warning bell; warning the voyager o'er life's tempestuous seas of the dangerous breakers and shoals; and many, by giving heed to that warning, escaped shipwreck, and have landed safely in the port of heaven. May that bell long sound the warning, and many yet, by heeding it, escape the danger, and be guided safely to the desired haven. Next came the Rev. Lyman, of whom we were not worthy, and his sojourn here was brief. And now our prayer to-day is, that our faithful beloved Miller may so distribute to us the bread of life, that each may receive a portion in due season, so that there may be no spiritual famishing here. But I have said enough, I fear too much. While then we look up in thankfulness to that Almighty being who has graciously lengthened out our lives to see this day, we ask you again, dear friends, to join with us in our thanks for all his mercies shown to us.

The choir then discoursed sweet music:—*Anthem.*

" Bless the Lord O my soul."

Dr. John Todd of Pittsfield, Mass., then gave one of his characteristic speeches. No report can do it justice. He referred to his leaving town fifty-eight years ago, bare-footed, and all his clothes under his arm. He recalled and presented before the mind of his hearers the old Church, and the customs of the people in those early days. He related many pleasing incidences which kept the audience in good humor.

It was a speech that must be heard in order to be appreciated.

Singing,—" What is Life."

After him, Gen. Wm. S. Pierson, of Windsor, grandson of Deacon Abraham Pierson, who was active in Revolutionary times, and who held correspondence with all the town boys who were in the field, having their letters to which he referred, gave the following

ADDRESS.

LADIES AND GENTLEMEN:

When I received the invitation from your Pastor, the Rev. Mr. Miller, to be present on this occasion, it was accompanied with the further request, that I should say something respecting my ancestors, who resided here for several generations; and also of the part taken by the citizens of this town, in the war of the Revolution.

These requests almost persuaded me to decline the invitation altogether; but when I came to think of the semi-centennial day of the dedication of the old Church, of which I had so often heard my father speak, I had so strong a desire to be here to-day, that I accepted the invitation to be present ; and on the still further request from your pastor, since my arrival, will address you for a few minutes.

Remaining a day in Clinton, formerly Killingworth, and part of this town, on my way here, and visiting the old Cemetery there, I found the grave-stone of my venerated ancestor, Rev. Abraham Pierson; and also the memorial stone, in front of the Congregational Church, of the founding of Yale College, of which he was the first Rector; by which I became reminded that he was a citizen of this town before the year seventeen hundred, as Pastor of the Church, and President of the College, until the time of his death; and also by the inscription on the grave stone of the son of the Rector, to the " Worshipful Abraham Pierson," I was reminded that he was an old Colonial Magistrate and Esquire, who lived a long and honorable life in this town; and then coming to Killingworth, and visiting the Cemetery of this Parish, I found the grave-stone of Deacon Dodo Pierson, who had moved from the South Parish at an early day, and passed a long life here, filling the offices of the town and church; and also that of the son of Dodo, Deacon Abraham Pierson, who was Treasurer of the School and Ecclesiastical Societies, Town Clerk, Selectman, Captain of the Military Company, Justice of the Peace for thirty-two years, Justice of the Quorum for Middlesex County for five years; and for twenty-four years representative of this town in the General Assembly of the State of Connecticut; and there being persons present and before me, who knew Deacon Abraham, I can but realize that it will be surely "like carrying coal to Newcastle," for me to attempt to say anything to this audience, about the old Piersons of the town of Killingworth. I will therefore say nothing further respecting this part of the request of Mr. Miller, than I shall have occasion, in speaking of the services of the soldiers of this town, in the Revolutionary war. Neither do I propose to speak generally on the subject of the part, our fathers in Killingworth took, in the war. Never having resided in this town, and indeed having resided out of the State most of my life, since my boyhood, some person more familiar with your citizens and local history, can better do justice to the subject.

I find, however, among the old papers which have been transmitted from former generations in our family, many letters, written to and from the soldiers in the field, in the Revolutionary war, and have brought a few of them with me, and will occupy your time a few moments in reading some extracts from them. These are the original letters, not copies even, and as they are genuine, will give a good idea of the patriotic sentiments of our ancestors, in that day of our country's trial. In looking over these letters this morning, the inquiry has pressed upon my mind, whether this town did no more than its share of service in the war, and if not, how great must have been the burden and the struggle of the whole country, in achieving our independence. North Killingworth was then a small Parish of the town of Killingworth, with a rugged soil, and sparse population, and still are found among the names of the soldiers in the field, the names of Redfield, Woodruff, Turner, Kelsey, Stevens, Hull, Buel, Bristol, Ward, Wilcox, Parmelee, Seward, Pierson, and indeed about all the names I have been accustomed to hear, as residents of this town. They were in the service from before the battle of Bunker Hill, until the capitulation at Yorktown, and the close of the war.

The first letter from which I will read, was written by Deacon Dodo Pierson. Both Dodo and his son Abraham were in the field; and it appears sometimes relieved each other.

New Haven, May 17, 1777.

Loving Wife and Children :

* * All the Continental troops are under marching orders for Peekskill, as we are informed the enemy are about to take the North River. We hear by a correspondence at head quarters in this town, that a detachment went from Ticonderoga in disguise, to St. John, and have burnt the stores. I am not uneasy ; our duty is not hard. I would not have my son attempt to supply my place until you hear further from me." You see the old man was good grit. When you hear a soldier say his duty is not hard, you may make up your mind he is a plucky fellow. I will only read from this letter one other sentence, characteristic of the man. " I desire that you would still maintain family prayers, that our separate ejaculations may still find audience at the Throne of Grace," and sends his " humble regards" to the Rev. Wm. Seward. It is a fact of interest, that almost every letter from the different soldiers, contains some message of respect for Mr. Seward.

The next letter, from which I will read a single sentence, was written by Ich'd Ward, to Abraham Pierson. It shows Mr. Ward's estimate of the services of the old man. " I believe that through the blessing of God, we shall have peace before long. I have seen your honored father standing sentry, which made me feel otherwise at first, but when I came to consider the grand cause he was in, I found myself rejoiced to think that men of his age and rank were willing to turn out ; and I hope God in his providence will return him to his family soon."

William Redfield, Jr., wrote from Camp 2d Hill, New Milford, that * * " It begins to be a little tedious, lying in tents these cold nights, and I should like to go home, but Capt. Lacy is not willing to spare me, and I must remain, if my country needs my services.

Eleazur Woodruff wrote to Abraham Pierson, from New York, Oct. 18, 1776, that * * " We are encamped on York Island, about eighty rods east from Mount Washington, in the woods. The place is universally liked—would not exchange places for any other regiment on the Island. We have good tents to live in, straw to lay on, salt pork and beef, good bread, plenty, and sometimes a few potatoes, cider at seven coppers a quart, and who can wish to live better than that." * *

With much experience with soldiers, I pronounce Eleazur Woodruff to have been a good soldier. He was no grumbler.

Abraham Pierson wrote from Camp North Castle, Nov. 10, 1776.

" HONORED PARENTS :

* * The first week after I came here, we were exceedingly fatigued. The enemy came within less than half a mile and daily hove cannon balls, which fell thick among us. A good Providence preserved all our regiment, though men were killed all around us. We were forced to lay on our arms, in an intrenchment night and day. One stormy night I lay out and was wet through. It was very cold. I could not dry my blanket the next day, and took cold. The enemy have gone back now, and we are more at peace. I have had the entire charge of the company, as there has been no other officer here." * *

Abraham Pierson also wrote from Camp, at Rye, New York, that * * "Whether I shall ever be so happy as to return home, the Lord only knows. Should I indulge in thoughts of home, perhaps it might cause discontent, but I am sensible it is necessary I should stay, and I am content." * *

We are all aware of the patriotic spirit exhibited by the women of our country, during the war of the rebellion, not only in providing for the wants of the men in the field, following them to the camp and hospital, and nursing the sick and wounded, but also in the greater sacrifice, perhaps, of encouraging their brothers, lovers and husbands to enlist, when they believed the country required their services.

This leads me to read a single sentence from a letter of Damaris Pierson, written from Killingworth, to her brother Abraham, when in the field.

* * "Father and mother desire to be remembered to you, for they are greatly exercised and troubled on your account, and desire to hear from you, and I hope you will come home, as soon as possible, without being very mean, for I greatly desire to see you." * *

This sister's devoted love did not induce her to ask her brother to do a mean act, in coming home, much as she desired to see him.

During the war of the rebellion, some of our men in the army, felt that unkind and unreasonable things were said by those at home. Human nature seems to have manifested the same depravity, in the days of our revolutionary struggle.

Ich'd Ward wrote from Camp Valley Forge, Jan. 18, 1778, to Abraham Pierson, * * "I am sorry to hear of the uneasiness there seems to be at home, concerning the soldiers. It seems, by what I can understand, that some are very uneasy because we have not killed all the enemy. They wonder what we are about—forty shillings a month—and nothing to do. I wish that some men were to undergo half as much as one of us has this winter, in long marches—lying on our arms, in open field and half starved. Now concerning our great wages, what expenses are we at for everything—half a crown for a quart of cider—one dollar for a pound of butter, &c.. Now what becomes of our forty shillings." * *

As early as Sept 11, A. D. 1775, Joseph Wilcox wrote to Abraham Pierson from Camp Roxbury, that * * "I am deprived of the privileges I enjoyed at home, and I know how to prize them, but I am willing to undergo anything, to preserve our rights and privileges to myself and others." * *

On the 22d day of February, A. D. 1776, Samuel Ward wrote to Abraham Pierson from Camp Roxbury that * * "We are ready to go at a moment's warning. We shall have a bloody battle, whenever we go there. I am very well contented to stay and fight for my country, for I believe it the duty of every man to come down, in this day of trouble. Our duty is very hard. No man that comes down here and sees the havoc these red dogs have made, can go home before he sees the country relieved from these rascals. For my part, I intend to stay and risk my life for my country. My life is dear to me, as any other man's, but my life is but a trifle to my country's liberty." * *

Ladies and Gentlemen—Was not Sam Ward a patriot?[2]

On the 2d day of October, A. D. 1775, Job Seward wrote from Camp Roxbury, to Abraham Pierson.

"My Worthy Friend:

When I think of home, I look over into Boston, and I see our enemy stand ready to slay every one of us, or to make slaves of us all, and I give myself contentment to be here, for if I know my own heart, I had rather risk my life in battle, than to risk my country and the many privileges of a sacred and civil nature, that we have enjoyed in times past." * *

Citizens of Killingworth, what think you of Job Seward? Are you not proud of your ancestors?

In times of great trial, moved by deep feelings and patriotic emotion, men from whom you would not under other circumstances expect it, express lofty sentiments, and perhaps in verse. As early as in seventeen hundred and seventy-six, Abraham Pierson prepared for the singing school some verses, which I will read, which were sung by the choir.

" O Liberty! how sweet the sound—
How dreadful is it to be bound,
In tyrant's chains—oppressed by those,
Who are our souls' and bodies' foes.

The sword is drawn against our land,
To make us yield to their command,
Which are unholy and unjust,
Therefore refuse them all, we must.

How far exceeds the martyr's death,
Who for his country spends his breath,
The life of him, who rather see,
His country bound in slavery.

O, may the God who rules above,
Look on our country, and in love,
Descend victorious, on our part,
That we may pierce the tyrant's heart.

May whigs have blessings, which may be,
Transmitted to posterity ;
May every tory ever dwell
Within, or near the gates of Hell."

During the war of the rebellion, it became my duty to command the Depot for confinement of captured rebel officers, to the
number of seven thousand. Among them were men who had
been members of the Legislatures of the different States—Judges
of the Courts of the State—Governors of the State—Senators and
Representatives in the Congress of the United States—Officers of
the Army, who had been educated at West Point, at the expense
of the United States, and men who had taken oath after oath to
support the Constitution, and yet all leprous with treason, and
dripping with warm blood, were captured fighting against the
United States; and when I saw the manifestation of their malig-
nant joy, at some of the reverses of our arms, in the dark days of
the war, I used to find myself repeating these last lines, which I
had learned in my childhood, changing the word tory to rebel :

May every rebel ever dwell
Within, or,

and I would stammer over the word "near," and I fear at the expense of the metre, and not having the charity of my old grandfather, leave it out, and leave these rebels without mercy, "within the gates of hell." But that day is passed, and we will all be magnanimous and forgiving now.

I said that deep patriotic emotion led persons sometimes to express their feelings in verse. This is true of another passion. Do the young ladies before me desire to know how the girls of this revolutionary period expressed themselves? If so, I will read for your especial benefit, and your grandmothers must not listen.

> " Your absence grieves me to the heart ;
> I cannot bear with you to part—
> For I with grief am sore oppressed,
> That night, nor day I take no rest.

> " You have my heart, oh sir, be kind,
> And leave another heart behind,
> And then shall I most happy be,
> When I your face with favor see."

No wonder Abraham Pierson wrote in verses. If such bright-eyed girls, as I see here, had written to me in this manner, when I was young, I am sure I should have imitated my grandfather in writing verses, however I may fall short in other respects. This letter is not signed by Lydia Redfield, my grandmother, and I may read the name of some other grandmother, unless you excuse me from reading the signature to this letter.

LADIES AND GENTLEMEN :

This is a great and glorious country, extending from the blue waters of Erie and Superior to the phosphorescent waters of Mexico; from the Atlantic to the Pacific; variegated and adorned with beautiful lakes and rivers, with extended plain and prairie, with grand old forests, with smiling valley and fertile hill and lofty mountain ; abounding in exhaustless mines of richest mineral and metal; embracing every variety of soil and climate and production; the broad savannas of the South furnishing the raw material, which, manufactured by the busy industry of the East, both the East and the South are fed by the overflowing granery of the West—all contributing to the common wealth and greatness. Under this free government of ours, our resources have developed with a rapidity of progress, such as the world has never before witnessed. The "desert has been made to bud and blossom as the rose." Where but a few years ago, in the beautiful language of Mr. Wirt, "in these lakes and in these rivers, the red man gathered his fish, and hunted his game," there are now the cultivated field, the thriving village, the refined and wealthy city. Instead of heathen rites and savage orgies, temples like yours have been erected, with spire pointing toward Heaven, dedicated to the worship of Almighty God. Our internal traffic is greater than that of any other nation; and our foreign commerce in the interchange of its commodities, in vessels with richly laden cargoes, propelled by that invention of modern days, of amazing power, in imprisoned steam, or by God's own breath against the white sail, seeks every port, in the fulfillment of its mission. We achieved our independence after a seven year's war, in which our fathers in Killingworth took so honorable a part; and years after we met the proud mistress of the sea on her own chosen element, and there caused our rights to be respected and acknowledged, wherever our flag floats from the mainmast in the breeze. While such was our proud position among the nations of the earth, and the philanthropist of every country and clime was casting his longing eye, to this "star of empire of the West," rejoicing that this free government of the people, was exercising such a beneficent mission among the nations of the earth, we found that our institutions were subject to another test. Constitutional government and constitutional liberty was then put on trial, and it remained to be seen, whether those institutions, which had been sufficient for the arts of peace, under which we had advanced to greatness and to glory; which had proved a sure defense against a foreign foe, would have a self-sustaining power, or whether we should perish by our own internal dissentions and divisions; by domestic feuds and border warfare; by treason and rebellion; until the name of our republic, like those of the old world, should only be known by its sad career, and bloody downfall; and our name, like theirs, become the argument of tyrants, for a further oppression of the subject. To put down such a rebellion, required the union of all loyal hands, and loyal hearts, and loyal means, and loyal men ; but we cut through every obstacle and institution, and every opposing race, or color of men, whether black, or white, or yellow, or red, till the majesty of our government was vindicated, and every where acknowledged.

In the gathering of our armies for this great conflict, the American Eagle, that proud bird, emblem of our nationality, hovered over them, in their encampment, and on their marches, and in the thickest of the fight; his bright eye flashing fire, as it caught our glittering guns, leading them onward, till victory perched upon our standard, and the stars and the stripes waving aloft, proclaimed the triumph of republican liberty. Then it was, that this nation stood forth as the great exemplar of equal rights to all mankind. Then it was, that it became true in verity and fact, as well as theory, in the language of the Declaration of Independence, that " all men are created equal—endowed by their Creator with certain inalienable rights, among which are life, liberty, and the pursuit of happiness." It was a prophetic vision of the greatness and glory and liberty of our country, which put it in the heart of Joseph Wilcox, while enduring the hardships of the field, in the Revolutionary war, to feel and say, " I am willing to undergo anything to preserve our rights and privileges to myself and others ;" and of Samuel Ward to say, "for my part I intend to stay and risk my life for my country. My life is as dear to me as any man's, but my life is but a trifle to my country's liberty." And of Job Seward to say, " If I know my own heart, I had rather risk my life in battle, than to risk my country and the many privileges of a sacred and civil nature, that we have enjoyed in times past." And of Abraham Pierson to say "I am sensible it is necessary I should stay, and I am content." Immortal honor to the memory of our patriot fathers !—Everlasting thanks for these patriotic words of theirs, which have been preserved to us until this day.

Rev. Mr. Bell, former Pastor, followed in a few remarks— showing that he had still an interest in the Church.

Hymn composed for the Anniversary by Mrs. Amanda V. Evarts, in the 74th year of her age :

HYMN.

Thy people long ago
  This house of worship rais'd,
O God of mercy, now
  Let thy Great Name be praised;
For sure this temple long has stood,
To shew the builders' zeal for God.

What wonders have been wrought
  Within this sacred place!
How many wanderers brought
  To seek the Savior's face;
Like the foundation ever sure,
The storms and tempests to endure.

The worthy men of God
  Who built this structure strong,
Now sleep beneath the sod;
  Their souls have joined the throng
Who need no earthly temple now
In which to praise as here below.

Who shall the story tell
  Of two score years and ten,
The mighty change reveal
  Recall the past again?
Ye who for half a century long
Within these walls have raised your song

As years have rolled around,
  God has his people blessed,
The Church His mercy found,
  Though oft with fear distressed;
• The Holy Spirit has been given
To lead repentant souls to Heaven.

Pastors to guide this flock,
  The Heavenly Shepherd gave,
Who lov'd the sacred work,
  And sought our souls to save,
And lead to Christ the living vine,
" Like stars forever shall they shine."*

From souls here born again,
  The news has spread around,
Of Jesus' love to men,
  The islands heard the sound;
From here COAN, beloved name,
With tidings of salvation came.

From hence that man of God†
  With great revivals blest,
Told of the Savior's blood
  To thousands East and West;
He now in Heaven, before the throne,
Ascribes the praise to God alone.

Dear sacred house of prayer,
  Within thy blest abode
May souls God's mercy share
  By his rich grace bestowed;
And still may every blessing flow,
For years to come, as long ago.

The meeting was closed by the singing of an Anthem by the Choir—and the Doxology by the Congregation.

BENEDICTION.

---

* Daniel 12, 3.   † Rev. Asahel Nettleton, D. D.

Thus closed a delightful day—a day long to be remembered by all who participated in its enjoyments, but especially by the members of this Church and Society, for the words of cheer spoken—for the happy social regathering of friends, and for the hope inspired that the future of this Church may be as bright—as honorable, as the past has been.

NOTES.

1.—Names of those who belonged to the Choir fifty years ago, and who sang at the fiftieth anniversary.

Mr. Rufus Redfield,	Mrs. Reuben Hinckley,	Mrs. Nathan Griswold,
Henry Hull, Esq.,	Mrs. Abel Wilcox,	Mrs. Ely Stevens,
Capt. Jerry Parmelee,	Mrs. Ezra Rutty,	Mrs. Hezekiah Child,
Col. Jedediah Stone,	Mrs. Jerry Parmelee,	Mrs. Rufus Crane,
Mr. Nelson Hall,	Mrs. Chauncy Parmelee,	Mrs. Alanson Lyndes.

2.—Residences of the first settlers.

Isaac Kelsey, Esq., lived on Cow Hill, a few rods east of Mr. Loomis's. Deacon Josiah Hull lived on Cow Hill, west of Mr. R. Hinckley's. Deacon Joseph Wilcocks lived on Tower Hill, just north of Col. Stone's. Daniel Buel lived where Mr. Sherman Stevens now lives. Joseph Griswold lived in the south west district, a few rods east of Mr. Nathan Griswold's. Nathaniel Parmelee lived near the house of Andrew Brooks. Ebenezer Hull lived near where Maj. Stevens now lives. Samuel Stevens lived on Tower Hill, near the house of Mr. Reynolds. Edward Rutty lived on Parker's Hill. Theophilus Redfield lived on Chestnut Hill.

3.—Names of the memorialists for a new Society.

Joseph Wilcox,	Peletiah Ward,	Theophulus Redfield,
Daniel Buel,	Lemuel Parmelee,	Ephraim Kelsey,
Benjamin Turner,	Nathaniel Hull,	Daniel Redfield,
Samuel Stevens,	Nathan Kelsey,	Nathaniel Wilcox,
Nathaniel Buel,	John Nettleton,	Matthias Kelsey,
Josiah Parmelee,	Nathaniel Parmelee,	Stephen Kelsey,
Abel Wilcox,	Timothy Chittenden,	Benjamin Carter.

4.—Names of the original members of the Church.

Edward Rutty,	Josiah Hull,	Elizabeth Hull,
Samuel Stevens,	Joseph Griswold,	Temperance Griswold,
Nathaniel Parmelee,	Benjamin Griswold,	Abagail Griswold,
Timothy Chittenden,	Joseph Willcocks,	Rebecca Willcocks,
Nathaniel Hull,	Benjamin Turner,	Martha Turner,
Josiah Parmelee,	Daniel Buell,	Elizabeth Buell,
Peletiah Ward,	Nathan Kelsey,	Hannah Kelsey,
Abijah Willcocks,	Abel Wilcocks,	Martha Wilcocks,
Nathaniel Buell,	Lemuel Parmelee,	Sarah Parmelee,
Daniel Rutty,	Jeremiah Stevens,	Concurrence Stevens,
Jonathan Hodgkin,	John Lane,	Experience Lane,

Daniel Lane,	Jemima Lane,	Jane Kelsey,
Nehemiah Parmelee,	Hannah Parmelee,	Ruth Willcocks,
Joseph Buell,	Anna Buell,	Elizabeth Roggers,
Jonathan Willcocks,	Experience Willcocks,	Remember Stevens,
Hannah Willcocks,	Priscilla Redfield,	Widow John Willcocks.
Bathsheba Clark,	Hannah Nott,	

Total,............50.

5.—Prices for other articles were as follows:

	£	s.	d.		£	s.	d.
Wheat per bushel,	0	5	0	Tallow, tried, per lb.	0	0	8
Rye " "	0	3	4	Wool,	0	1	6
Indian Corn, "	0	2	6	Flax,	0	0	7
Oats, " "	0	1	6	Butter,	0	0	9
Beef, per cwt.	1	0	10	Cheese,	0	0	5

6.—Names of College Graduates:

William Seward,	Aaron H. Kelsey,	Martin Wilcox,
John Punderson Seward,	William S. Pierson,	Luther Hull,
Asahel Nettleton,	Alvin Parmelee,	Sylvester W. Turner,
Philander Parmelee,	Josiah Pierson,	John Wilcox.
Henry Lord,	Ebenezer H. Wilcox,	

Two, also, while pursuing their studies at Yale College, died:—" Ely Kelsey, son of Aaron Kelsey. He died April 26, 1788, aged 25 years, wanting thirty-two days."

" A vigorous application to the Academical studies, early finished a life devoted to learning and religion. His benevolence and integrity, and his exemplary piety endeared him to his friends, to the seminary and to the church of God, and enabled him to die in so heavenly a manner, and to recommend religion to all, and make every one wish to have died in his stead.

In Christo, mea vita latet; mea Gloria Christus, in uno Jesu omnia."
Written by President Stiles.

Reuben Wilcox : "College Education partly completed; died in the morning of life, Nov. 18, 1788, aged 24.

Youth blooming: Learn your mortal state, how swift your life, how short the date.

Via lethi ab omnibus tentanda."

7.—Names of those who have entered the ministry:

William Seward,	Philander Parmelee,	Titus Coan,
Asahel Nettleton,	Martin Wilcox,	John Wilcox,
Josiah Pierson,	Henry Lord,	Eben. H. Wilcox.
George Coan,	Alvin Parmelee,	

:S.—Number of admissions to Mr. Coan's church, from 1837 to 1863:

1825 to 1837	84	1851	169
1838	539	1852	192
1839	5244	1853	442
1840	1499	1854	176
1841	154	1855	95
1842	273	1856	83
1843	331	1857	105
1844	306	1858	81
1845–6	553	1859	48
1847	117	1860	51
1848	186	1861	106
1849	265	1862	72
1850	164	1863	57

Total,............11,491.

www.ingramcontent.com/pod-product-compliance
Lightning Source LLC
Chambersburg PA
CBHW021517090426
42739CB00007B/649